LEARN TO CODE. GET A JOB.

VERSION 2

GWENDOLYN FARADAY

CONTENTS

Cover Designer: Faith Miller, Faith Miller Designs

Editors: Ali Solomon, Daniel Lomelino, Carol Faraday

Publisher: Faraday Publishing

This book is an original work of Gwendolyn Faraday and conveys the opinions and experiences of the author alone. Nothing in this text is meant to give legal or financial advice.

ISBN-13: 978-1-7340044-2-7 (Paperback edition)

ISBN-13: 978-1-7340044-4-1 (E-Book edition)

First Printing: 2019

Second Printing: 2020

Current Version: 2

Created with Vellum

ACKNOWLEDGMENTS

I am grateful to my friends and family for their help in proof-reading and editing this book, as well as giving me ideas and inspiration to keep going.

Carol Faraday

Daniel Lomelino

Fish & Kitkat

QUOTES

"To me programming is more than an important practical art. It is also a gigantic undertaking in the foundations of knowledge."
- Grace Hopper, Computer Engineering Pioneer

"Most good programmers do programming not because they expect to get paid or get adulation by the public, but because it is fun to program."
- Linus Torvalds, Creator of Linux

"Self-education is, I firmly believe, the only kind of education there is. The only function of a school is to make self-education easier; failing that, it does nothing."
- Isaac Asimov, Famous Author

FOREWORD

Between thousands of different learning resources out there and myriads of tools for learning to code, it can be very overwhelming for someone just starting out.

How do I get started?

Which resources should I use?

What's the best way to learn?

When will I be ready to look for jobs?

How can I get hired?

There are so many questions to answer that many people waste a lot of time just studying up on learning methods and then end up giving up in frustration. In the last several years of running a local group that teaches coding skills, I've seen many people give up because they are overwhelmed by the amount of choices and information available.

This book is intended to make sense of all the madness and give you a simplified step-by-step approach that you can follow to prepare for a job as a web developer or any other type of programmer. Useful resources and encouraging stories are linked from the appendices as well as sections throughout the book.

I really hope you enjoy this book and find it helpful.

If you have any feedback for me, please reach out.

Gwendolyn Rose Faraday

PREFACE

I have always had an interest in building software applications – both for the web and other devices. I built my first website almost 18 years ago using Yahoo's Geocities, which allowed HTML styling and a few layout choices. After that, in the early 2000's, there was the Myspace era, where you could customize your profile layouts by tinkering with the code. I thought it was the most amazing thing that I could create so many things without using physical materials; just by writing code.

When I went to college, I enrolled in engineering and studied Matlab and C++. I also had fun building GUIs (graphical user interfaces), websites, and RPGs (role-playing games) outside of class.

You may think that I would go on to a life as a software engineer and have a great career after that. Unfortunately, that was not the case. I lacked many of the fundamental skills necessary to work as a professional. It's not just about building websites. Being able to build quality software means learning the necessary patterns, tools, and frameworks to work collaboratively with a professional team.

I spent years taking course after course and keeping up with the latest online learning content. I learned so many technologies at a basic or sometimes intermediate level and then would move on to the next shiny new thing that people were telling me I should learn. I can't even recall how many tutorials I started and never finished or how much time I wasted in research that never amounted to learning a useful, practical skill.

I had a passion and desire to be an application developer but I never had a current, hire-able skillset and I had no idea how to market myself to break into the industry. I worked in many other fields, including management, sales, food service, and IT – a lot of these jobs were somewhat low-paying and stressful; usually with long hours, too.

I had one major problem holding me back from the career I really wanted: **I never had an organized plan, path, or goal.**

Fast Forward to 2015

As I so often do, I started the year with ambitious goals to change my life, get in shape, and work toward a more fulfilling career.

By the end of 2014, I had completed a TeamTreehouse-.com learning track for building IOS apps in Swift and I had a portfolio of three working mobile apps! I was so excited that I decided 2015 was—without question—the year I would definitely become a software developer!

The Plan

I quit my time-consuming job as a salesperson and got a temporary job at a local restaurant for 35-40 hours per week, which freed up a lot of time for me to research and study. I immediately began to make a plan for what technologies I would learn and how I would learn them. I decided to focus on web development, figuring I could easily switch back to mobile or something else later on.

To build modern web applications, there are so many tools to learn. I was motivated and excited to start but couldn't quite figure out where to begin. I was entertaining the thought of going to a coding bootcamp to jumpstart the process but it was expensive and I would have to take months off of work with no guarantee of a job afterwards. I thought about going back to college for Computer Science but I didn't like the idea of waiting years to graduate, spending a lot of money, and having to self-study a lot anyways because the curriculum would be years outdated (colleges take years to approve and implement new curriculums and update material, which isn't ideal for technology that changes every day).

I scoured the internet for free and paid resources and made huge lists over the next several months. I was spending an inordinate amount of time on just research! I needed some structure and a guide. Around May of that year I found just that.

I came across a free online curriculum to learn HTML, CSS, and JavaScript called freeCodeCamp. It gave me a structure and path through what to learn and had me build a portfolio of apps as I went along.

It was my good fortune that around the same time I stumbled upon an audiobook called, "No Degree, No Problem" by Josh Kemp. The author used to shoe horses for a living and then taught himself to code and landed a job in about eight months. It was so inspirational to hear his story that I listened to it over and over again to stay motivated.

Over the next few months, I spent as much time as a I could working my way through the freeCodeCamp curriculum. I made a pledge that I would only learn what was included in that curriculum to avoid going down too many rabbit holes (a very easy thing to do on the internet).

In June of 2015, I started a local group to network with, and help, other people who were also going through this amazing journey of learning to program. That local coding group has grown to be over 1,200 members while hosting around 100 meetups and events over the past five years. Wanting to expand our programs, in January of 2020, with the help of a small team of other software developers, I officially launched a non-profit, free coding school to help members of the community learn web development skills in a structured classroom setting (now online, due to the Covid-19 situation).

Long story short, after networking and studying for at least three hours per day, I landed my first job. That was in October of 2015. I've been in love with this career ever since.

Between my own experience and working with so many other self-learners, I have acquired a lot of insights that I want to share in this book. I hope people can use what I have learned to help change their mindset, career, and maybe even their path in life.

What to Expect from this Book

This book is divided into five sections:

1. Information & Planning
2. Learning
3. Networking
4. Job Preparation

5. Getting Hired

The book begins with advice for planning and studying; and then provides information on how to choose or create your own curriculum to serve as a pathway for achieving competence as a programmer, building a portfolio, and landing your first professional job. In each chapter, you will find action steps to start working on right away, as well as advice on what to expect throughout your learning journey.

The third section includes tips and advice for putting yourself out there. It includes on- and off-line methods of networking with other people and how to get as much exposure as possible.

The final sections get into the nitty gritty of landing that tech job. It's a long road but this will give you a glimpse of the finish line and how to get there. Consider this your guide for how to handle recruiters, job applications, and maximizing your chances of getting job offers.

The information in this book has been edited to ensure that it's easy to digest and understand; however, since you will have to review much of it over time, each chapter is a stand alone guide on a particular topic for easier referencing.

Terminology Used in this Book

- I use the terms **developer, coder, programmer,** and **software engineer** interchangeably in some areas of this book. They all mean pretty much the same thing and you will notice this when you start to look at job descriptions. If you write good code, adhere to best practices, and concern yourself with stability, security, and performance; you are a software engineer or any of the above.

- A **meetup** refers to an event where people get together to hear a presentation or discuss a certain topic. They are usually held in-person and may be connected to a national/international organization or run by a group of locals passionate about a certain topic.
- Sometimes, I use programming-specific terms like CSS, SQL, HTML, JavaScript, etc. If you don't know what something like that means, do not worry, it is not important for understanding this book. This is a technology-agnostic guide so knowing specific languages or tools is not necessary.
- **Tech stack** refers to the languages, technologies, and related tools used in a specific project or company.
- **Repository** (repo) is a place where the files and folders of a piece of software are hosted online. Storing code in repositories makes it easy to share with other people and include on your resume, among other benefits.

Important Information

The resources mentioned in this book can be found at: gwenfaraday.com/learn-to-code-book.

You can reach out to me with questions or concerns related to this book at gwenf@protonmail.com. I usually respond to emails once a week, so it may take at least a few days to get back to you. For faster response times, please join my Discord chat community of like-minded learned and developers: https://discord.gg/FYbdFHq.

A list of errata and updates from this book can be found at: gwenfaraday.com/learn-to-code-book/updates.

If you find this book helpful, please leave a positive review so other people can benefit from it as well. If you find any part of this book to be in error, please let me know via email: gwenf@protonmail.com.

Why don't I include the learning resources inside of the book?

Technology changes very quickly, and software is no exception. While books are a great way to convey ideas and teach certain things like software patterns, some material just doesn't age well without frequent updates. Programming languages and tools fit into this category. The right way to do something six months ago might not work today.

Another consideration I have taken in deciding the content for this book book is keeping it relevant for a broad audience. Not everyone has the same goals or is going to learn the exact same skill set. You will notice that I make recommendations of what to learn first to help beginners avoid the paradox of choice; however, if you have a different goal in mind, like learning robotics or IoT, this book will still be useful.

These are the reasons I have chosen to include the concepts and explanation in this book and use a different medium to house the related and recommended learning material.

INFORMATION & PLANNING

Section 1

1

RECOMMENDATIONS FOR STARTING

I want to start this book off with some general recommendations for how to get started. If you ask people for advice on learning how to code, you will be given many different answers for what to learn and how to learn it. Much of the advice you will receive will not be wrong, but it can be overwhelming when you do not know what the best option is. The truth is, there are many different flavors of programming and much overlap between them all. It is not bad to learn one language over another or one style over another.

In this chapter, I will cover some general recommendations I have for getting started as well as frequently asked questions that you may have. The recommendations I make here are based off of the assumption that you are new to programming and need some help getting started. Once you land your first job, you can steer your career in whatever direction you fancy.

First Steps

No matter what path your career takes, there are some basics that you will need to learn first. I just want to give you an overview of the starting point up front, with more details being covered in the next few chapters of this book:

1. You need to understand the options available to you for software development jobs.
2. You need to choose a specialty; what type of applications you are going to build or ecosystem you want to work in.
3. You need to choose a language.
4. You need to create a curriculum.
5. You need to make a study plan.
6. You need to take action.

Those are the steps that it takes to get started on your journey which we will cover over the next several chapters of this book. You can worry about everything else - networking, building a portfolio, job hunting, etc. - after you have a plan and have already started learning. These topics are all covered in future sections of this book. Let's dive into step one now.

Overview of the Flavors of the Software Development Industry

The field of software development is not just about being a coder; there are hundreds of verticals you can work in and thousands of ways to specialize in the industry. Let's take a high-level look at some of the work environments and job options available to you. Keep in mind that all of these jobs and company types do overlap quite a bit and these are just generalizations.

Types of Companies

The atmosphere at companies can vary greatly depending on the type of company and industry. While you may not have the luxury of being overly selective when searching for your first role, you should take the time to thoroughly research the company to see if the role and company aligns with your ideal workplace and values.

Tech Companies

Companies whose primary products are software or hardware applications are called tech companies. They include companies of all sizes but Facebook, Apple, Amazon, Netflix, and Google - called the FAANG companies – are some of the most well-known. I would also include two other renowned tech giants, Microsoft and Salesforce, on this list.

There are a few notable differences between working at tech companies versus non-tech companies. In my experience, tech companies usually appreciate their software developers more and give them more freedom to be creative and innovate. They are usually more receptive to adopting modern technologies and are often forward-thinking about the changing tech landscape. Additionally, tech companies are typically more open to hiring employees with non-traditional backgrounds, such as self-taught developers and coding school graduates.

There are small considerations I want to mention that you may not find in a job description. The developers I know who work for large non-tech companies in industries like finance or healthcare, usually have a business casual dress code (definitely no t-shirts or jeans for them!). and must adhere to a set schedule that requires them to be at their desk during regular business hours. If those two factors aren't a part of your ideal work environment, consider if there are other company benefits that outweigh them or if the company can offer you any flexibility in those areas.

At times, in non-technical companies, the needs of the business and bottom line overshadow the technical expertise and potential offered by a team of developers. Sometimes businesspeople are even put in charge of technical decisions. These companies traditionally don't embrace the 'get your work done whenever' attitude like many modern software development companies where their employees and developers are given flexibility and many perks.

In my opinion, most people would enjoy working at a tech company, small or large, over a similarly-sized non-tech company.

Corporations

Corporations include large companies with at least 1000 employees. Some benefits of working at these types of companies are that they have dedicated budgets for training, pay larger salaries, have plenty of opportunities for growth, and look great on your resume

At large companies, however, your contributions may not be as impactful. As a developer at a large corporation, you will have a very specialized role and may start to feel like a cog in the wheel churning out lines of code.. It can also be challenging to obtain an entry-level role at corporations because of their more formalized education and experience requirements. Many of them will reject candidates who don't have an engineering or computer science degree. Your best opportunity for getting in the door is through networking with employees to get a referral, or with internal recruiters who can help expedite your interview process.

If you're given the opportunity, I highly recommend working at one of these companies when you are starting out. Even just a year of gainful employment at a large corporation will make the rest of your career and future job searches easier. In the unlikely event that you're laid off before your one-year anniversary, chances are you'll get a decent severance package that will support you while you look for a new role.

Mid-sized companies

Mid-sized companies are the most stable and conservative option, and have anywhere from 100-1000 employees. They are small enough that they can better support their employees on a more individualized basis, and aren't large enough to push for growth beyond the sustainability of the company.

One perk of working for a mid-sized company is the flexibility they offer their employees; however, they do not usually carry the brand recognition or weight as the experience gained at a large tech company or corporation.

Startups & Small companies

Start-up companies usually have less than 100 employees and have only been in business for a few years, making them one of the most volatile types of companies to work for. . The majority of all startups are venture-backed and are pushing hard to return a profit or grow quickly, sometimes at the expense of their employees. Startups are far more likely to either scale quickly or become acquired by a larger company..

Another factor to consider is that some startups are just a group of self-funded co-founders making a cool product, but these are less common and generally have fewer than 20 employees.

Personally, I worked for a self-funded startup with about eight employees and it was one of the best decisions I made in my career. I was able to get one-on-one mentoring from someone who had been programming for decades and was very patient with all my newbie mistakes. I definitely recommend working for a startup or small company that is not just pushed to grow and keeps the well-being of its employees and stakeholders at the forefront. These companies only grow larger if it makes sense, not solely because of investor pressure.

There are, of course, downsides to working at these types of companies. The most common one is long work hours. Startups often require non-traditional hours and lots of commitment from early employees in exchange for growth opportunities and equity. Another drawback for smaller companies concerns their finances. Sometimes their budgets are so tight that they have to wait to hire more staff or invest in more company resources, and they can be less organized if they do not have a dedicated Finance or Payroll department.One company I worked for was routinely late with paychecks because of an overworked boss who let it slip his mind. If you're the kind of person who wants routine hours and a stable environment, this might not be for you.

Because of their size, there are many opportunities to

take on responsibilities outside of your everyday role. This can be a great opportunity to learn what you like and get extra experience, but it can also lead to more stress and longer work hours. Make sure you are up front with during the interviewing and onboarding processes regarding the hours you are willing to work and any accommodations you might need.

If you're considering working for a small company or startup, oftentimes open positions aren't posted on online job boards. One reason for this could be because they may not have the budget for Human Resources personnel, or they don't want to pay to advertise on with job sites like LinkedIn or Glassdoor. This is an instance where networking and keeping up with industry trends becomes just as important as having a killer resume and the right skill set (don't worry, we'll cover all that later).

Consulting agencies

Consulting agencies vary by size, but deserve a category all their own.

Most of the time, if you work for a consulting agency, you will switch projects every six months to one year and will get to work for many different bosses on a plethora of technologies.Reputable consulting companies will let you change projects when you start to feel bored or burned out, which is great if you're a lifelong learner. For some personalities though, it is more stressful to have to frequently onboard a new project and tech stack within a relatively short timeframe. Before considering this option, so you should do some research on the agency and industry to see if it's right for you.

There are two main types of work you will do at a

consulting agency: staff augmentation and outsourced projects. Here are some details about each one:

1. Staff Augmentation

In most cases, you'll work with a team of internal employees onsite at a software company, or a company that specializes in another product but has some programmers on staff. In the latter case, because you'll be working alongside a company's employees, they will usually be stricter in enforcing rules like adhering to a certain dress code or set schedule.

Another thing to keep in mind when working for a third-party company as a consultant or contractor is that even though you may be doing some of the same job duties as a regular employee, the company you are doing the work for has no legal obligation to offer you the same benefits as someone who is a direct hire. This means that you might not be able to take part in the same activities that everyone else on the team does, like participate in company sports or group activities or attend certain training opportunities. This type of work environment can become isolating but know that there's almost always another opportunity to go work for a different client and team, minus the awkward goodbyes and separation paperwork.

2. Outsourced Projects

Generally, this will entail working internally with other employees of your consulting agency and is preferable to staff augmentation because you're working directly for your employer without the middleman. Your client will be whatever company hired you to build or update their app, and you'll usually be placed with senior developers that you can learn from and can show you the ropes.

Types of Developer Jobs

There are a few different types of jobs available to developers, and it is a good idea to know a little bit about each so you can set your goals appropriately.

Internal employee

Full-time or part-time employment is the most common type of job you will be searching for.In the United States, this is known as a "W-2" or "regular" employee, meaning you are hired directly by the company and they are responsible for paying taxes and providing benefits like health insurance, paid time off, and retirement plan options Keep in mind that if you're searching for part-time work, you may not be eligible for the same benefits as a full-time employee.

On average, it costs a company around $30,000 to hire a developer, so the company has an interest in keeping you happy. Perks of being an internal employee include mentorship, free training or conferences, and opportunities for professional growth. If you make a mistake or need some extra help, most companies will do their best to support you, making direct hire roles much more secure than being a contractor or outside consultant.

Even though these jobs offer a lot of stability, they can become monotonous, especially if you're not given a lot of autonomy in making decisions. The tech stack that you start with is likely the one you will work in for the foreseeable future at the company. If you find you are getting bored or burnt out, you may be able to fix the problem by talking to your supervisor and asking for more responsibilities outside of your current role or potentially transferring to another team or project. If it still does not improve, you can seek other opportunities elsewhere after your first year of experience.

Consultant

Generally, consultants are viewed as industry experts with a wealth of experience in a certain profession or industry, but this outlook is not necessarily true anymore. Anyone who is hired by a company to solve a specific problem or fill a need can be called a consultant, regardless of your years of experience. If you are freelancing on your own or working for an agency as a subcontractor, you can call yourself a "software consultant"; which sounds much better on your resume than a "freelancer."

Contractor

While it may be tempting to work for yourself, being a contractor is not for everyone. Contract work can be less stable, and you will have to pay self-employment taxes and continuously sell yourself and your skill set to keep getting projects. You will spend extra time keeping track of hours and billing clients, and it is likely no one will be there to mentor you as they are expecting a certain level of expertise right away.

If you need flexibility and don't mind the extra time spent on administrative tasks and relationship-building, this might be the right choice. You can take only the projects that you want, and if you happen to work with a client or project that was not particularly enjoyable, you can choose not to work with them again. Contracting work is especially good if you are becoming an expert in something that has a large demand and you really like doing it (like building iOS or Android apps or cloud development).

Software Verticals

Lastly, I want to give you an overview of the main types of software development that you might want to work in. This will also give you an idea of keywords that you can look for when researching job postings.

- Web Development - Front-End: Do you already have an eye for design and want to learn development? Front-end positions may be a good place to start. In these roles, you will primarily focus on the user experience and design aspects of the platform, working primarily in browsers using languages like HTML/CSS and JavaScript to build user interfaces. There is some overlap between UX design and front-end development.
- Web Development - Back-End: Are you more interested in the logic of an application than the user interface? For back-end development, you will work directly in the code, and not a browser or emulator. You will also need to pick up some related skills like SQL/NoSQL and the Linux Command Line.
- Full-Stack Development: Do you enjoy elements of both the front- and back-end development? Full-Stack, or "web development" means that you know, enough to be functional on a team in both areas. From experience, most of the jobs

requiring full-stack skills are mostly front-end-focused, with some light back-end work.

- User Interface/User Experience (UI/UX): UX/UI developers are sometimes also called web designers, and work almost exclusively in front-end development. Many companies confuse these terms when they are trying to hire developers with this skill set, and their roles usually include non-technical components like doing research and having a fundamental, yet iterative, understanding the customer's psychology to help cultivate the user experience.
- Wordpress Development: It is easier to get a job doing this type of work than some other development roles, but it will usually lower-paying and will not leave you with the most in-demand developer skillset. However, if the right opportunity arises, it can still be a good entry-level job for getting started in the industry.
- Cloud Engineer: If you get certified by one of the top platforms like Amazon Web Services, Google Cloud, or Microsoft Azure, you can get lots of great jobs working on the cloud. This type of job is much like a development role where you have to solve problems and manage software applications, but takes place on the infrastructure side, meaning most of the code you write will be for deployment scripts and managing resources instead of building applications.
- Embedded Systems and Desktop Applications: These positions require lower level knowledge

about computer languages and hardware, which can be harder to learn when you are starting out.

- Native or Cross-Platform Mobile Development: These roles are similar to front-end mobile development, but are exclusively for phones and tablets. You will probably pick either iOS or Android to specialize in or focus on making cross-platform apps that work across devices.
- Database Administrator: These jobs involve managing and optimizing database interactions. This is a well-paying position that can also be a good entry point for a developer position. Many companies would love to hire a developer with strong database skills.
- Quality Assurance (QA): QA pros are basically professional software testers. Depending on the company, you may write tests in code or spend much of your time clicking around a user interface and handling tickets. This can be a good entry position to lead up to getting a developer job because they generally have a lower barrier to entry, but they also pay less.
- Cutting edge industries: Working in a specialized industry like IoT, Artificial Intelligence, Machine Learning, Blockchain, or self-driving cars require higher levels of math and development experience, making them more difficult to get into initially.
- Gaming: There are many types of companies that build games: large game companies, mobile gaming, indy companies, etc. While not all gaming-focused companies do this, this industry has a bad reputation of mistreating their

employees with long hours and high stress for low pay.

Some people want to work in a specific field or industry and others love building a certain type of software. The type of job you want might change as you go so do not worry about picking one just yet. We will discuss choosing a vertical a little later in the book.

Let's move on to some frequently asked questions.

What Language Should I Learn First?

Before you choose a language, set some goals and do your research. We will cover language selection in a few chapters.

Should I Specialize or Be a Generalist?

I hear this question often, and unfortunately, the answer isn't black and white. If your goal is to find a job as quickly as possible, you have to be flexible enough to pick up whatever new technologies an employer might use. On the other hand, if your skill set is too broad, you will not have anything of substance to show off in your portfolio and employers might view you as too junior to be hirable.

What I recommend is **Specialize** in one language and a few frameworks (one or two) and tools to go along with that language, and **Generalize** in the ecosystem that you are working in (e.g. web development).

Why use this approach? From my experience, putting these recommendations into practice allows you specialize enough to be able to build robust applications in your chosen language and ecosystem, resulting in a more impressive portfolio. It also gives you confidence in your coding abilities, making you appear more professional on job applications and in interviews. Companies will see you have practiced and developed your skills in one language enough to achieve some level of mastery. Having deep knowledge of one language is much better than shallow knowledge of several.

Should you specialize in frameworks and tools as well? Yes, pick a few of each and stick with them. Ideally, when you are starting out, you will pick the most popular ones so you will be able to have a large community to help you if you get stuck and need help. Knowing at least one popular framework can really help you later on when you are looking for a job as well.

Being a generalist in the ecosystem means that you will be staying up to date on all of the developments and new things happening around you, like innovations in web development, mobile development, or IoT. You specifically want shallow knowledge here for the purpose of gaining a broader perspective of advancements in your field without wasting time or feeling burned out (this happens a lot with the pace of change in technology). Knowing your ecosystem well is essential to becoming an expert, and also looks great when you are in job interviews. You do not have to know how to implement the latest and greatest tech trends, you just have to know how to talk about them. I give some recommendations later in this book about staying up to date with the tech world.

What if I Need to Learn a Different Language or Ecosystem for a Job?

Once you know how to program, you can become proficient in any language with just a few weeks of full-time, focused study. In the event that you do need to learn a new language for a job, that's okay, go ahead and apply.

When you are interviewing for specific jobs that do not fit perfectly in your chosen tech stack, spend a few hours going through tutorials and learn a little bit about what they are using, enough that you are able to pick out some keywords and concepts while you are interviewing with them. If you do not get that job, go back to your regular curriculum and tech stack as soon as possible.

Whatever you do, do not fall into the trap of thinking that the specific language language you are studying is better than another language, or look down on another style of development. Programming languages are just tools for building applications. If you learned JavaScript and a company wants to hire you to program in Python or PHP, you should seriously consider the job anyway. If you learned one language, you will already be ahead of the curve on learning another. You will almost certainly be programming with a new tool or in a new way when you take a job, and rather than be intimidated by it, try to embrace it embrace it as a new challenge.

The only caveat I would say here is make sure you aren't getting in over your head. If you enjoy design and desire to work in front-end web development, but then are offered a back-end position, ask yourself if you are okay with putting in the extra effort of studying and doing that for at least one year. Getting your first job is difficult, so while you must be flexible, you also have to be honest with yourself about your personal needs and capabilities.

Specialize as much as you can in order to become proficient in a language and set of tools while you are learning. Try to understand underlying programming concepts and patterns as you are studying. This will help you generalize as needed when you are looking for a job. Do not be afraid to venture into new languages when a company shows interest in you.

Additional FAQs can be found in my Discord chat: https://discord.gg/FYbdFHq.

Beginning is Great

> "The beginning is the most important part of the work."
>
> — Plato, The Republic

The goal of this book is to make you hirable as soon as possible. Once you get hired, you will have plenty of time and support to develop your skills on the job. Most tech jobs do not require a degree or deep knowledge of math or computer science, they just want to see a baseline level of technical ability and your desire to continue to learn. You can demonstrate all of this by building out a portfolio.

When launching a product, the goal is always to get to the minimum viable product (MVP) state as soon as possible. This allows much more leeway for iteration and making tweaks to the product as it develops. It's the same with learning to code.

Start coding as soon as possible! Don't spend too much time researching or learning theory, jump in and learn as you go. If you wait too long, you are probably going to procrastinate and/or burn out. If you get stuck, it is a good sign that you are pushing yourself. Stay focused on the end goal where you are paid well to learn and challenge yourself every day!

2

COLLEGES VS CODING SCHOOLS VS SELF-STUDY

"I have never let my schooling interfere with my education."

— Mark Twain

There is no one right learning path for everyone. Different types of learning can be beneficial depending on your circumstances and personality, and what works for some may not work for others. Some -learners will pursue a college degree or get formal training for certifications after they have been working in the field for a few years, while others may jump straight into a coding school after or during high school.

Here is a breakdown of the pros and cons of the three most popular methods for learning programming skills: college, coding schools, and self-learning or self-study.

College

The college route is considered the "traditional" method for becoming a software engineer. It most commonly consists of acquiring a bachelor's degree in computer science or computer engineering. The curriculum focuses on math (usually Calculus 1, 2, 3 Differential Equations, and statistics), and includes some general education, science, and computer topics like application and hardware architecture, programming design patterns, and may include a few different programming languages.

Getting a bachelor's degree is a long-term investment (typically three or more years), and many adults cannot put their lives on hold to go to college full-time, not to mention it is. I expensive and requires you to take courses that may not be directly applicable to your career path. Computer science programs have a statistically high dropout rate for a myriad of reasons ranging from boredom to incomprehension. College professors are also self-taught in many ways, have to keep up with trending technologies on their own, and may or may not have experience in the industry.

If you do choose to go back to school, I recommend majoring in software engineering or computer science, despite their reputation. These degrees will give you the best shot of finding a job afterwards. There are many new degrees for IT and related tech skills, like Bachelor's of Cloud Computing, but they usually have far fewer requirements and do not hold the same weight in the industry. If you are going to spend the time and money going to college, you might as well get the highest quality degree that you can, whether that means taking community college courses and transferring to a four-year university later, or jumping headfirst into an accredited program. Before you enroll, discuss your intentions with family, friends, and trusted connections who want what's best for you, and choose your college and curriculum carefully.

Pros

- College is considered the standard approach, and some companies prefer hiring candidates with computer science degrees. Having a bachelor's degree may expose you to other opportunities that you wouldn't have otherwise qualified for.
- You will learn a lot about underlying computer systems and architecture.
- Colleges usually have resources to connect you with industry professionals and companies in your area where you can gain some practical advice and experience.
- Many colleges offer training for industry-standard certifications as part of their coursework. Depending on the type of software development you go into, this can really give you a leg up in your job search.

Cons

- Many college curriculums do not prepare students adequately for the workforce. They teach the underlying principles but not the technologies that you will be working with every day. As a result, you will have to learn a lot on your own regardless.
- Some accelerated and adult bachelor's degree programs can be completed within three years,

but on average it takes anywhere from 4-6 weeks to graduate if you do not already have credits.

- The curriculum might be outdated due to the rapidly changing technology industry. Creating new curricula is expensive and colleges can take years to approve changes to them.
- The average computer science bachelor's degree in the United States costs more than $150,000 – a price that is well beyond what many of us can afford.
- Most people are in debt when they graduate, college, regardless of the school attended. Even with the help of financial aid and scholarships, sometimes takes years or decades to pay off the full price of a degree.

Coding Schools

While coding schools (commonly called coding bootcamps) cost less than college, they can still be prohibitively expensive. Since most of them require 40-60 hours per week of classroom work, plus homework, it is almost impossible to work full-time while attending one of these programs. Additionally, they must be completed within a set timeframe without any flexibility, which can make it challenging to learn the material at such an accelerated rate. Some more reputable coding schools heavily screen incoming students to make sure they possess a certain level of technical knowledge before enrolling.

There are some concerns about the lack of regulation and the variable quality of the curricula. Some of these schools have even turned out to be scams so it is extremely important to do lots of research before signing up for one.

Many coding schools have also been known to exaggerate job placement claims (I have witnessed this myself) and may say things like "95% of students land jobs within four months of graduating." That sounds great on the surface, but they may be including students who were placed in non-programming jobs like tech support or who are working for a tech company in a non-technical role.

There are good coding schools out there but, because of the hype and lack of regulation, you need to do your due diligence and assiduously vet them before enrolling. If you are looking into this option, please talk to current or former students and teachers and review the curriculum and claims thoroughly.

Also know that you need to be prepared *before* beginning the program. I have mentored several students during and after attending coding school programs and there is a clear distinction between the students who prepared beforehand and those who didn't (or only did the minimal amount of prep work assigned). If you can, it is best to practice for 5-10 hours per week months before the program starts to make sure you have the basics down. I've seen some students unable to perform simple programming tasks even after 12 weeks of coding every day because they failed to understand the fundamentals and had to quickly progress through the rest of the coursework. This can make or break your ability to find a job afterwards. If you are interested in pursuing a coding school, I have some helpful information linked from the resources for this book on my website.

Pros

- You may be able to land a job within 3-6 months of graduating.

- Some coding schools have very good mentorship programs and job placement opportunities.
- This might be the best option if you need a directed, classroom environment.
- Bootcamps usually teach you current, in-demand skills and how to use tools that you will use on the job.
- Part-time and remote programs are available in some cases.
- Some coding schools offer alternative payment options such as taking a portion of your salary once you find a job. This helps to align the school's goals with your goals as a student— they are incentivized to help you learn and find high-paying jobs.

Cons

- The cost of one of these programs can range from $12,000-$25,000. Even if the program allows you to defer your payment until after you've graduated, there are still your living expenses to consider during the program and while you are job searching.
- There is no job guarantee! Even coding schools with job guarantees do not have 100% placement and will refund your tuition if they do not place you.
- The learning environment is usually fast-paced and intense. Not everyone can be successful in that type of environment.
- You need to prepare and do at least a few months of self-learning to succeed.

- If you agree to do an income share where the coding school takes a portion of your salary for a few years, they can require that you to take the first job offer you get, even if it is not a good fit for you. Sometimes, they will also offer you internal jobs that are just over the income minimum so you might have to work for a reduced salary for the coding school itself for a while to fulfill your agreement.

Self-study

Forgoing formal education is becoming more and more common every year. An excerpt from the largest yearly developer survey reads, “Developers are lifelong learners; almost 90% of all developers say they have taught themselves a new language, framework, or tool outside of their formal education.” Not only that, but about a quarter of all professional developers do not have a college degree (many successful and well-known ones are on this list). I personally never graduated from college or attended a coding school program, though I am considering going back to college to pursue some software engineering research opportunities.

Being self-taught is a bit of a misnomer because the majority of the content has a teacher behind it. The term “self-study” seems to fit better here. Nowadays, there are several free and low-cost content available with experts and teachers from various backgrounds to choose from.

The main drawbacks to self-study are having to stay motivated, networking on your own, eliminating distractions, and formulating a curriculum.. Fortunately, there are many people like myself, who have been through this process and are there to help. It is incredibly daunting to create a curriculum, which is where the self-motivation comes in. You will need to commit to both a plan and a goal and keep taking steps forward even when you feel frustrated, uncertain, or unmotivated.

Some of the benefits of self-study are learning at your own pace and having flexibility for where and how you choose to learn. It is also, by far, the cheapest of the three options. You can choose to sign up for subscription sites with video courses on various topics (~$25 per month) or buy a few books. Other than that, the cost comes down to time, elbow grease, and grit. It a great option for students with families or lives that cannot be put on hold, or those who cannot or do not want to spend an excessive amount money to achieve the same outcome. There is also a benefit for companies; by When companies consider candidates with non-traditional backgrounds, a whole new world of potential diversity opens up for them, benefitting everyone involved.

Pros

- The cost is minimal, depending on what materials you decide to purchase.
- You can learn whatever topics you choose at your own pace, when and where you want.
- There are lots of people out there who will mentor, help, or advise you for free.
- Teaching yourself is great for building skills like knowledge acquisition and problem solving.

Cons

- There is no instructor directing or guiding you.
- You will have to find your own curriculum and

stay motivated to finish it (this book is here to help you with this problem).
- You have to overcome all of the distractions around you on your own.
- Networking is necessary and completely up to you to follow through on.

Conclusion

If you choose to enroll in a formal education program, you will still have to teach yourself many things. If you decide to self-study or go to a coding school instead of college, you could end up with a job within your first year of learning. This would allow you to get a few years of real-world experience in the same amount of time that you would spend pursuing a degree. Remember, the number one thing most tech companies look for is experience, not a college degree. A degree helps you get your foot in the door, but your skills, experience, and how you are using the knowledge you learned is what matters most.

In the end, only you can decide which choice is right for you. While this book focuses on teaching yourself, many of the concepts are relevant no matter which option you choose.

Action Steps:

1. Select the pathway that works best for your situation: college, a coding school, or self-study.
2. Spend some time doing research, but do not spend too much time stalling. Make a decision and stick with it.

3

RESEARCH & PLANNING

"If you fail to plan, you are planning to fail."

— Benjamin Franklin

As I've stated previously, you need to have a learning strategy and well-developed plan before you start programming. One of the top reasons why people give up on their coding journey is from failing to plan their pathway. This is precisely why it took me years to buckle down and get to the point where I was hirable as a developer. Please learn from my experience and take some time to map out your path first.

This chapter will cover some basic steps you should take before putting together your curriculum and diving into the code.

Step 1: Finding Your Why

Knowing *why* you want to learn programming is the first step in your journey. You might be thinking, "That's easy! I want to get a good job and make lots of money." While those are great goals, those reasons alone lack emotion, and feelings are what drive our actions. You need to take a step back to figure out what is beyond your mission-oriented goals to discover your real motivations, because that is what will keep you going when you want to give up.

Simon Sinek, author of *Start with Why* and *Find Your Why*, recommends that in order to find your 'why', you should ask yourself lots of 'what' questions instead of 'why' questions because they are easier to answer. Try starting off with the following questions:

- What gets you out of bed in the morning?
- What makes you want to be a software developer?
- What kind of life do you really want to live?
- What would your ideal day look like when you are working as a programmer?

Every time you write an answer, you should naturally come up with more questions. Keep going until you start to uncover the emotions underlying your reasons. This process should take less than 30 minutes if you are completely undistracted.

If you are a creative or crafty person, you may want to create a vision board to remember their why. Or, you could do what I did and create another version of this where I hung a motivating picture on my fridge or next to a quote and a list of my goals and why statements. I like the simplicity and constant visual reminder of my intrinsic motivations and what I want to accomplish.

Please do not skip this step! If you do not do this now, you may find it challenging to communicate your purpose or goals to others when you are looking for a job or stay motivated in the long term.

Step 2: Industry Research

To get to the point where you are fully ready to set goals, first you need to do some research on your own. The purpose of this step is to help you understand what types of jobs are available and what technologies you will need to learn to get hired for one of those jobs. Job markets can vary by location and company type, so learning one set of technologies is not right for everyone.

First, start writing down some information that you already know about your wants and needs in a job position. Here are some good questions to get you started:

- Where do I want to live (if open to relocation)?
- How far can I commute?
- What salary and benefits do I want?
- What are my ideal work hours?
- What kind of environment do I want to work in?
- Is there a vertical I am drawn to in the tech industry - mobile apps, websites, etc.?
- Based on the information in Chapter 1, is there a certain company environment I would prefer working in?

It may seem trivial to write down things you might already know in your head, but, from my experience, this is a very important step to help you realize what you actually want out of a job. *Be sure to distinguish the job factors you want to have from those that are non-negotiable.*

Once you have the above information, you can start to

research and find companies that come as close to what you want as possible. How do you research for these jobs? Use whatever job websites are popular in your area. Here are some ideas to start with: Indeed, Glassdoor, LinkedIn, Github Jobs, Stack Overflow Jobs, government job boards, and language or technology specific job boards (e.g. Vue Jobs). If you know of any companies in your area, you can search their websites' career pages for postings as well. You can also attend local meetup groups and ask other professionals in your network about which technologies are the most in-demand in your area, but take these kinds of recommendations with a grain of salt. Individuals are usually biased towards the specific tech stacks that they work in.

What terms should you be searching for on these websites? Words or phrases like software developer, web/mobile developer, software engineer, and programmer. Look at the job details and bookmark or save links to any jobs that fit your criteria. Do not worry if the requirements do not match your current skill set or years of experience the purpose of this exercise is purely for research. As you dive in, seek out positions that include the word "junior" and skip over any that say "senior" or "lead", they might have specialized skills that you will not need to learn until later on in your career.

Once you have a solid list of positions that interest you, highlight the technologies, languages (Python, JavaScript, C#, Swift, etc.), and any relevant terms that are listed in the job details or requirements section. You will see that there are several commonalities between most of the job postings.

Now, take a look at the Stack Overflow survey (the current one is from 2020 - https://insights.stackoverflow.com/survey/2020#technology-programming-scripting-and-markup-languages-professional-developers) and compare the languages you see on the survey. Most of them should be on that list. If any language is not on the Stack Overflow survey, or is at the very bottom, I recommend removing it from your list. In that case, that particular language is very likely company-specific and will limit your job options if you pursue learning it. You can do the same thing to narrow down your choices of frameworks, tools, and databases: go to the link above and replace the hashtag and words after it with, #technology-web-frameworks-professional-developers2, #technology-other-frameworks-libraries-and-tools-professional-developers3, and then #technology-databases-professional-developers4. Keep removing any of the less popular tools and technologies from your lists until you are left with a few items in each category.

Once you have your chosen few languages, take note of which ones you saw the most often in the job postings that fit your criteria. Write down the number of times next to each item if you can. These lists will be the basis for your curriculum.

Step 3: Goal Setting

The third step is to write out your goals. You do not need goals for your whole career, but you do need an idea of what type of job and company you are looking for so you can customize your learning and portfolio accordingly. After reading the previous chapters and doing some of your own research, you should already have the information you need to write out your goals.

It is very common to change your mind as you try out different types of programming and figure out what you like to do. As you learn more, your goals will likely evolve and change over time, and that's okay! The most important thing is that your goals align with your "why" statements..

When thinking about your goals, consider your answers to the following questions:

- What kind of apps do you want to make?
- Do you want a job in the industry or work for yourself? What kinds of things are you passionate about: education, cutting-edge technology, robots, fashion?
- How much money do you need to make?
- How many months/years do you want (or need) to accomplish this?

You should review your goals every time you feel unmotivated to study or experience any other of coding's many frustrations. From my experience, many people consider giving up from time to time and remembering your goals and your "why" - or having someone else who can remind you of them - can be what keeps you going.

For me, there came a point in my life when I knew that I was fed up with myself and my situation enough that I was going to achieve my goals no matter what. I let the people close to me know what I was setting out to do and I felt accountable to both myself and them to pull through. I had a bad track record of quitting in the past, so I made it a point to set goals and broadcast them on my blog and elsewhere to help me persevere. With where I am now, I am so happy that I did.

Step 4: Choose a Stack

It is time to choose a tech stack! What language, frameworks, and tools do you want to start learning? Your mission as learner is to become as much of an expert as possible in one tech stack: Learn one programming language, two frameworks, one database (if you are not learning only front-end), and whatever tools are necessary to build apps in those frameworks. *For example, if you are going to learn Python, then you might want to choose to learn Django and Flask as your frameworks and Postgres as your database. If you learn full-stack JavaScript, you might choose to learn Vue or React as well as Node.js with a standard back-end framework like Express. If you only want to focus on the front-end, then you could learn both Vue and React and dive into some UX and layouts instead of a database.*

Which one should you choose? You will have to ultimately decide that for yourself, but here are some tips I have compiled from my experience:

- **Mentorship:** If you are one of the lucky ones who already has friends or family who are willing to help you learn, then sometimes the best option is to start learning whatever language and type of development that they can teach you from their experience. For example, if your cousin is a C# developer and willing to teach you how to code, then pick up C# first. You will receive invaluable training from a professional who works in C# every day.
- **Specific Goal:** If you are in the group of people who has a specific goal in mind, such as, "I want to build mobile games," or, "I want to learn web

development," then you should learn the most popular language and tools to help you achieve that goal. For some types of games that means learning iOS' Swift or Android's Kotlin or, maybe, C# for PC gaming.

- **Freelancing:** If you want to be a freelancer for anything beyond simple websites, I recommend that you work at a tech company first for at least a year. This will give you real-world experience in how tech is used and it will be much easier to build client projects and find better clients to begin with. Also, I recommend taking a freelancing course, like one I took by Real Tough Candy. (I am not sponsored, but I have gone through her freelancing course in the past). Remember that freelancing is language-agnostic. You can learn any language and tools to be a freelancer, and will become an expert in whatever area of development you choose.
- **Job Market Demand:** You may be fortunate enough to live or have connections at certain companies in an area that has a shortage of a certain type of developer, like PHP, C#, or something similar. This is may be music to your ears and could be a good opportunity for getting your first development job. If you decide to base your learning on what's in demand, make sure that the programming language and tools you are learning aren't too niche. That might cause problems for you if you end up having to broaden the scope of your job search. Always try to learn a general purpose, popular language first. It will provide you with your

greatest chance of success starting out in the industry.

- **Other:** If you do not fall into one of the above categories, here's my advice for you. Based on experiences of members of my coding group, my own countless hours of research, and trial and error, I recommend learning the language JavaScript first. It is, compared to many other languages, easy to learn, versatile, and includes a wide range of job opportunities from building mobile apps to full-stack web development.

Benefits of Learning JavaScript & Web Development First

> "Any application that can be written in JavaScript, will eventually be written in JavaScript."
>
> — JEFF ATWOOD, CODINGHORROR.COM

Because I just recommended JavaScript, I want to cover some of the reasons why. Like I mentioned above, there are a lot of programming languages and a lot of people who will tell you to learn one over another. Comparatively speaking, most of them are not better or worse than one another, they are simply different. With a barrage of competing opinions, it is not easy to pick just one, and, if you heed everyone's advice you will get nowhere.

In case you weren't convinced, here are some facts about JavaScript:

- **Popular:** For seven years now, JavaScript has

been ranked the most popular programming language in the world by a wide margin (source, Stack Overflow Developer Survey 2019). – Note: I'm only comparing JavaScript to other general purpose, standard programming languages.

- **Versatile:** JavaScript is really ubiquitous now. It is popularly used for building web, mobile, TV, and desktop applications and for server-side development with Node.js. It can also be used for building various IoT devices, for smart homes, automation, robotics, etc., and you don't have to be good with design to learn JavaScript, although that option is available .
- **Beginner-friendly:** It is one of the easiest languages to learn as it abstracts a lot of the complexity of what goes on inside the computer (memory, threading, etc.) away from you. On top of that, you can use it right away in simple web pages and see your code run in the browser, giving you instant feedback that can help you build your confidence and better understand how the code works.
- **Community:** JavaScript has a massive community comprised of millions of people from all over the world. It is the largest and most active online community according to Github's yearly report, providing you with extensive learning materials, mentors, and other resources.
- **Jobs:** Every company that does anything with the web uses JavaScript, which is virtually all of them! Most companies that use Python, PHP, Java, and other languages also use JavaScript.. According to Indeed, the world's largest job

search platform, JavaScript is the second most hirable programming language (this information is based on 2018 job search results from Indeed.com).

Once you learn one language, it is much easier to learn the second since you already know the concepts of programming. I used front-end development with JavaScript as an entry point into the field and then moved on to programming various types of applications in several different languages. I eventually wound up doing machine learning and working for a blockchain company. There are many companies that will hire you as long as you have experience in any language, regardless of what their in-house tech stack is.

I want to reiterate that this book contains a roadmap for people learning to code and is language-agnostic. If you choose to learn a different language and other technologies, that is totally fine, just do not waste time wallowing in indecision. Pick a language and ecosystem and stick with it. Learn, get a job, and then set a new goal.

Conclusion

Action Steps:

1. Write down your "why" and put it somewhere you will see it.
2. Do some industry research.
3. Use that knowledge from your research to set goals.
4. Choose a tech stack to learn.

4

CODING CURRICULUM

Now that you have chosen your language and stack you want to learn, you need a curriculum to guide you.. You have two options for this: you can create your own or select a pre-defined curriculum that has already been created. This chapter will show you how to select or create your curriculum, start planning, and take action.

Step 1: Create an Ordered List

The first thing you should do is look at coding school (or "bootcamp") curriculums that teach the same stack you are trying to learn. This is a good first step because their sole focus is getting students up to speed and "job ready" in as little time as possible, and can help you build your learning plan, self-directed or predefined.

Here are a few recommendations (sometimes you will have to enter an email to be able to see their whole curriculum):

- App Academy (appacademy.io)
- Thinkful (thinkful.com)
- Grace Hopper Academy (gracehopper.com)
- Springboard (springboard.com)

As you review them, take note of what technologies they teach and the order they teach them in. You will probably want to keep the same order for your own curriculum since they usually laid out from easiest to hardest. The material should also be layered and will likely build on the initial material.

If you are learning full-stack web development, for example, your keyword list could look something like this: Node.js, Express.js, Vue.js or React.js, HTTP, REST, MySQL, Sass/CSS, HTML, Git, and Webpack. Your curriculum should also include most, if not all, of those items.

Step 2: Choosing a Curriculum

Option A: Choosing a Pre-Defined Curriculum

Let's start with the easiest option and the one I recommend: choosing a predefined curriculum (or multiple curriculums consecutively). Below is a list of quality coding curriculums, and, remember that you might have to use multiple to get to your learning goal. Fortunately, many of the popular free and paid curriculums online have reviews from other students going through the same process that can help offer insight into the materials and overall program.

Free Options:

- **freeCodeCamp:** This is a project-based

curriculum with thousands of hours of content for learning Python and JavaScript.

- **Open Source Curriculums on Github:** There are some great curriculum options in Github repositories that compile lists of free resources to take you through bootcamp or degree-equivalent programs at your own page. Here is an example of a do-it-yourself Computer Science degree from Open Source Society University: github.com/ossu/computer-science. You can search Github.com to find more.

Paid Options:

- **Coursera Specializations:** These are a series of courses taught by accredited universities that cost about $39-$49 per month to take. I recommend checking out the Full-Stack Web Development with React or Android App Development Specializations. They have many other good ones as well.
- **Team Treehouse:** Their tracks are very well-structured for beginners, and they have a broad range of different technologies covered on their platform. You can also try out one of their Tech Degree programs, which has more structure and support than their regular website.
- **Udacity:** If you need to learn something more cutting-edge like machine learning or robotics, then I recommend looking at syllabuses from the Udacity nano-degree programs and seeing if any of those meet your needs. I have found them to

be in-depth with well-presented course materials.

- **Udemy:** I recommend checking out the Complete Web Development Bootcamp by Angela Yu. She is an excellent teacher and the course takes you all the way from the very basics of HTML to building your own full-stack JavaScript projects with React. There are lots of other good, comprehensive classes on Udemy as well. The good thing about this site is that you can see reviews and ratings from thousands of other students and you also get a "no questions asked" 30-day return policy.

Both the free and paid curriculums I mention above can be robust and high quality, and, in my experience, have proven beneficial for new programmers. Sometimes paying for your education can be a good motivator to push through and complete the courses, but you can choose what's right for you and your budget.

Option B: Creating Your Own Curriculum

Creating your own curriculum is more time-consuming, but might be required if you are trying to learn emerging technologies or something specific. The best way to do this efficiently is to take your ordered list of technologies and research the best resources to learn each individual topic.

Here are some helpful websites with beginner-friendly courses, videos, articles, books, and interactive coding challenges to supplement your learning:

- No Starch Press

- Pluralsight
- Front-End Masters
- College course sites like Coursera and EdX
- Khan Academy
- Code challenge sites like Hackerrank and Codewars
- Mozilla Developer Network Guides and Tutorials
- Launch School's Open Library (launchschool.com/books)
- LinkedIn Learning
- Udemy
- SoloLearn
- Talk Python to Me
- Microsoft's Learning Paths (docs.microsoft.com/en-us/learn)

If you choose this route of creating your own curriculum, do not spend more than a few days on it before you start coding. Find courses or other materials for each topic and move on to the next one. If you start going through a course and do not like it or cannot understand it, then just replace it with another one and keep going.

Much of your learning should come through building projects. In software development, these projects are called applications. Once you have a list of learning materials, write down one project to build for each topic, and know that some projects will cover multiple technologies and concepts. As you build out your projects, try to utilize every concept you learn to practically apply your newly-gained knowledge. If you spend a lot of time studying without applying the material, you will easily forget what you learned, plus getting your hands dirty makes learning more enjoyable and rewarding. It feels amazing when you see something you've created after many hours of hard work.

I recommend going through just a few lessons, then jumping right into a project. This is a good pattern to maintain throughout your learning: go through a few tutorials, videos, and articles, then jump right in to building your own project. The process will look something like this:

Tutorials for Learning New Concept X

1. Tutorial 1
2. Tutorial 2

Practice Concept X

1. Project 1

Tutorials for Learning New Concept Y

1. Tutorial 3
2. Tutorial 4

Practice Concept Y

1. Project 2

Note: the time it will take you to complete each project will increase as they get more challenging and complex.

If you are stuck not knowing what projects to build, take a look at websites or apps that you use and try to build a clone of one of them. You can also look at portfolios or curriculum from coding bootcamps to see what projects those students are building. Since this is for learning, the idea doesn't have to be novel, just the code to build it. *There are also some project recommendations on my website, linked from the resources for this book.*

Step 3: Adding Supplementary Material

There are certain concepts that you will need to know beyond learning a tech stack like design patterns and algorithms (basic and intermediate, no need to get too advanced). I think these are absolutely essential for being successful in the industry. Algorithms teach you problem solving skills and how to think in code. I cover this a little later on in the book, but I want to include resource recommendations here to include in your curriculum.

- Get an account on a website like codewars.com and practice going through their coding challenges at least once a week. Start with the most basic ones and keep pushing yourself to get better.
- Go through Harvard's CS50 course on EdX. It is excellent at teaching programming basics and you can choose to pay $90 for a certificate or audit the course for free. I recommend starting this near the beginning of your learning and doing it in parallel with the rest of your curriculum.
- Depending on what you are learning, you may need to brush up on your math skills (especially if you are learning Data Science or a field of AI). Khan Academy, Coursera, and Brilliant.org all have excellent math courses with practical exercises.
- Whatever you do, make sure you learn Git and

Github. You will need this skills for any job and even for working on your personal projects. Try. github.io is a great place to learn all of commands you need to know for using these tools, plus it is free! I created a free course for freeCodeCamp's YouTube channel on this topic.

- Learn a code editor well. I recommend Microsoft's VS Code for starting out. It is beginner-friendly, free, and is used professionally.
- You cannot learn one language alone, you need to learn the ecosystem. No matter what type of programming you do, you will need to learn a set of tools and related skills. I recommend that everyone learns some command line skills as a programmer. My favorite book on this topic is *The Linux Command Line* from No Starch Press. If you are doing web development, you will also need to the developer tools available to you in modern browsers. All languages have some kind tooling available to you for debugging.

Conclusion

Action Steps:

1. Create a list of technologies to build your curriculum.
2. Select or create your own curriculum.
3. Make sure it includes building projects to practice your skills.
4. Add in supplementary material like Harvard's CS50 course.

5

PREPARATION FOR LEARNING

Learning to code takes more than just a creating a curriculum to follow. This chapter will guide you through preparing systems, setting aside time, and organizing your digital and mental space for learning to code.

Time Calculations

How long will it take to learn to code? That depends on many factors, including what you are trying to learn, where you are starting from, your ability to focus, your ability or willingness to network, and how much time you can spend every week.

One thing to remember is that there is no definite amount of time to learn. Books or courses that say, "learn this language in 24 hours" or "become an XYZ language developer in one month" are laughably unrealistic. You must go at the pace that you can handle while creating a solid foundation of programming skills for yourself. Take your time and learn the fundamentals well-- it will pay dividends.

The first step is deciding how much time per week you can allot to your learning. Consider that you will probably need 700-1000+ hours of total learning time to become proficient enough to get a job, so if you study roughly 20 hours per week, it could take about 9-12 months to land your first role.

Once you calculate the hours, break it down and compare it to your original timeframe for reaching your goal, then ask yourself if that is reasonable or not. You might have to adjust your hours accordingly.

Next, take out your calendar and block off that time in your weekly schedule as the "no matter what, I am doing this" time, and structure it to suit your needs. You could block off a few hours per day, or do longer chunks on your days off or during the weekend, or both. If you cannot spend at least 10 hours per week studying and coding, it may be very difficult for you to become skilled enough to land a job in a reasonable amount of time. *I am not trying to dissuade you from learning if you have less time to spend, but I want to help you set your expectations correctly.*

If this is something you really want to do, you will make the time. I know parents who worked multiple jobs who taught themselves to code, and know that you can too, no matter what your situation. When I started, it took me years of dabbling to finally focus my efforts and commit to what I wanted to do. Once I dedicated over 20 hours per week studying, my career took off very quickly.

Note-taking

It can be incredibly helpful to take notes while you learn so you can document your "aha" moments and keep track of what you are learning so you can review it later. Coding involves many complex processes, and without regular review, it is difficult to retain all of the concepts.

You should take notes as you learn in just *one place.* Many students have both paper and digital notebooks with notes in each of them, which can make it extremely hard to stay organized. To get the most out of your time, I would strongly recommend keeping a digital notebook where you can sort and search entries, and store relevant links like video tutorials and images such as diagrams or screenshots. Here are some digital note-taking option::

- Evernote - cross-platform, great free tier
- Bear - Mac only, $1.99 per month, very easy to use, beautiful interface
- Joplin - free, privacy-focused, cross-platform

Another option, and what I have been using recently, is using a tablet with a pen like an iPad or Surface pro. These allow you to handwrite notes, organize them into folders, and still search through text. I also like that tablets make it easy to draw diagrams and illustrations while I am writing, so it's the best of both worlds.

Spaced Repetition Learning

This is an optional step, but can be a great addition to note-taking. Wikipedia's definition of spaced repetition is "a learning technique that incorporates increasing intervals of time between subsequent review of previously learned material in order to exploit the psychological spacing effect." This concept consists of sets of digital flashcards that are shown to you more often if you are struggling and less often if you are getting them correct (you self-select if you got the answer correct, of course).

When I was starting out, I felt overwhelmed by the material, and spaced repetition learning helped me immensely in retaining the information I was learning. It especially helped me during interviews when I was asked about my understanding of technological concepts and terms. I even surprised a few interviewers with my compelling verbiage.

There are many spaced repetition learning programs and apps, so find the one that works best for you. These are the ones I have personally tried and recommend:

- Ankiweb (ankiweb.com)
- Mem.dev (https://mem.dev)

One great thing about these flashcard decks is that they are shareable. If you create decks as you go, go ahead and post them online for other people to learn from, too. It is a great feeling to be able to give back to the community even while you are just starting out.

Planning Sessions

To stay on target, you will need to have periodic planning sessions throughout your learning process. I personally use the methodology from the book, *Getting Things Done* by David Allen. He details how to set aside time for weekly and monthly planning, as well as clean up your to-do lists. If you do not want to read the book, here is a simple breakdown of how to effectively plan.

1. Block out a time every week when you know you will be available and without distractions. It usually takes me about an hour to do my planning, but you can adjust the time depending on your preferences.
2. Each week, you should look at the list of things you have to learn and plan what you are going to try to accomplish for that week.
3. Throughout the week, you will come across many concepts you do not understand, topics you are interested in, or other random to-dos. Instead of letting all of these "extras" distract you, write all of them down in an "inbox" in one of your digital notebooks or list apps.. During your next weekly planning meeting, you will want to review these inbox items and put them on your to-do list for the week, toss them, or put them in a "someday/maybe" pile.
4. If you have monthly planning sessions, that is a good time to go through the "someday/maybe" pile.

Study Sessions

Every time you sit down to study, you should already know what you are going to be doing according to your plan, which is a huge time saver. It can easily take 30 minutes or more to get your mind in gear and figure out what to work on if you have not planned properly, and that could be an extra 3.5 hours each week you could have spent studying.

Planning is important at the beginning, but when you are wrapping up each session, it can be very helpful to keep a short project log. This log is the place for you to jot down a few short notes about what you worked on that session, any struggles you had, and where you left off. This gives you peace of mind so you can close all of your tabs in your browser and your mind without worry. Your project log will be there the next time you sit down to code and you can pick up right where you left off instead of spending extra time reflecting and trying to remember exactly what you went over the last session.

If you are a tab hoarder like me, it might be useful to create a bookmarks folder for coding and then use the option "bookmark all tabs", which is available in all modern browsers. You can use this method to save all your tabs in a bookmark folder arranged by date or topic for easy reference later.

Study sessions can be any length of time, but it is best to make them at least an hour long to account for ramp up time – things like setting up your computer, opening the right applications, getting in the zone, etc. If you have less than an hour to spend, it might be better to catch up on your backlog of articles and videos, or go through individual challenges on sites like freeCodeCamp and Code Wars.

While you are studying, it is extraordinarily important to stay focused, which can be challenging knowing that distracting websites are just a few clicks away. If you find yourself getting distracted while you are studying, try using a browser blocker plugin like StayFocused (Chrome) or LeechBlock (Firefox). You can set the amount of time you want the distracting websites blocked for, and even schedule weekly block times. Some of the websites I regularly block are social media sites like Twitter and Facebook, email clients, and forum sites like reddit. If you find yourself heavily distracted by apps as well, I recommend trying out Freedom - which is what I currently use - that blocks apps and web traffic across all of your desktop and mobile devices.

If you have trouble focusing, I highly recommend reading the book, *Deep Work: Rules for Focused Success in a Distracted World,* by Cal Newport. He tells about his personal journey to learn to focus and gives practical advice for building up the amount of time you are able to focus for. Having the capability to focus for several hours at a time - sometimes called "being in the zone" - is extremely important as a software developer. You will be trying to solve technical problems in creative ways, which is not easily done when you're unfocused.

TIP: Timers and the Pomodoro Technique

Motivational speaker and productivity guru, Mel Robbins, has a wildly successful campaign called "The Five Second Rule" where she encourages people to simply start counting to five every time they do not feel motivated to complete a task. Why is this simple act so popular and successful? Because timers work. Research shows that if you do not feel like doing something, you can start a timer for a few minutes, and once the timer finishes, you are almost guaranteed to continue working on or finish the task at hand. This works because you see results which give you a rewarding feeling in your brain along with a renewed sense of motivation, thus, making you want to keep taking action to receive more positive stimuli.

The Pomodoro technique is a method of setting a timer

for a certain timeframe, traditionally 25 minutes, and then taking a break for a shorter amount of time, usually five minutes. Forming a habit where you are focused for an amount of time, then take a break can lead to increased productivity. You can play around with the amount of time to see what's right for you. Personally, I used to set my work timer for 50 minutes and the break timer to 10 minutes. Now that I have an Apple Watch, it goes off every hour to remind me to stand up and walk around so I only use my timer for work and I never stop it until I'm done or need a longer break. If you search online for Pomodoro timers, you will find plenty of options that you can use for free.

Digital Organization

You will find out quickly that you need to have folders on your computer for photos, code files, and related items. It is good to come up with a labeling system and naming conventions for your folders and files in the beginning so you can easily navigate them as you go. I have one master folder where I put all my coding projects called "code", and have various trees of subfolders for different types of projects and computer languages. I also keep client work separate from personal projects.

You can create whatever file structure works for you, just make sure to do it early on. It is also a good idea to schedule time every week to look over your notes and clean up anything that is out of place or irrelevant.

Motivation

When aspiring developers go back to school or enroll in a coding bootcamp (and spend a lot of money to do so) that alone can be enough to motivate them to study and persevere. In a more formal program, they will usually have a mentor there to push them along, but in the case of self-learning, however, you may need extra help staying motivated. Here are some suggestions:

- Keep your goals and "reasons" where you can see them often. This could be near your study area, on the fridge, or written on a greaseboard.. I had sticky notes all over my apartment to keep me focused on my goals while I was learning.
- You can make friends with people who are also learning by going to your local coding meetups, or finding online groups to participate in. Some really good ones are freeCodeCamp (local meetups and awesome online community), Girl Develop It (yes, it is for guys too), and Coder Newbie (online community). I link these and many more in the resources for this book on my website.
- Don't do it alone! Find a group or an accountability partner in one of the previously mentioned groups. You can check in on each other asynchronously so you do not have to schedule meeting with each other every week. The important thing is consistency.
- Announce what you are doing online to help keep you accountable and working through times when you want to give up.

- Put some money where your mouth is. Pledge to donate a sum of money if you fail to meet your goal or sign up for an accountability app that will donate your money for you. Money is a great motivator but it doesn't have to be just cash: it could be a chore or anything else depending on your circumstances.
- Read the suggested materials in the motivation section on my website when you need a pick-me-up.

TIP: Avoiding Burnout

Psychology Today defines burnout as, "a state of emotional, mental, and often physical exhaustion brought on by prolonged or repeated stress." Burnout is when you feel drained and lethargic, like you cannot continue. Sadly, this is a very common occurrence in programming so do not feel like you are alone if it happens to you.

If you do start to feel burned out, I recommend that you take a step back and review how you are spending your time. If you are overworking yourself, put some parameters in place to achieve better balance depending on the root cause of the burnout. If the problem comes from coding problems that you are struggling to solve, take a break from that and work on a different activity. If you are building an app for example, start working through some coding challenges like the ones on HackerRank or reading some coding articles. This will offer you the opportunity to mentally distance yourself from the frustrating situation, but still be able to improve your overall knowledge and coding skills. Feelings of burnout should be taken seriously and handled appropriately, or your mental health and ability to stay focused and motivated will suffer.

Some other tactics I employ when I feel burned out is to schedule walks throughout the day where I focus on my breathing and leave my phone at home. I also like to watch motivational videos - especially Arnold Schwarzenegger ones on YouTube - to help me regain my drive.

Unless you make the decision that coding is truly not for you, keep learning and persevering, even if you need to slow your pace. If you get burned out and do not handle it properly, then you might quit learning to code before you have given it a real shot, which I think would be a tragedy.

Conclusion

Start off with some simple planning and organize your notes system, inboxes, etc. and do not feel overwhelmed by the amount of preparation and material to learn. Do not forget to participate in the community and read through the motivational resources on my website, or reach out to others when you need some encouragement.

Action Steps:

1. Calculate the total amount of time needed.
2. Figure out where and how to take notes.
3. Use spaced repetition learning.
4. Schedule planning and study sessions.
5. Use motivational techniques when necessary.

LEARNING

Section 2

6

LEARNING THROUGH BUILDING

"By bringing real-life context and technology to the curriculum through a project-based learning approach, students are encouraged to become independent workers, critical thinkers, and lifelong learners."

— Edutopia.org

Projects are critical to your coding journey because they are the visible proof of what you have learned. Every project you build will go into your portfolio and can be talked about on your blog and social media (more detail about this can be found in later chapters). The first few projects are for ramping up your learning and gaining practical skills. As you build more advanced applications, you should be spending increasing amounts of time polishing the details because those are the ones that will remain in your portfolio when you are looking for a job.

This chapter contains advice on for planning, building, and finishing projects.

Project Planning

It is tempting to start building and start building projects in the code right away. While this is fine for your first small project, it is not sustainable. Every project should start with a goal and user stories, then a list of requirements and simple mockups, and finally have a list of actionable tasks. This will help you get used to a systematic approach that you will be using as a professional. It is a good idea to keep all of these planning documents and mockups from your projects to show off on your blog or, potentially, when you apply for jobs.

As you are planning, keep a minimum viable product (MVP) mindset. In other words, figure out the minimum number of features you can include in the initial build of the app. You should write down each piece of the app that you have to build and keep it in a task management system. I recommend using Trello for this step because it is easy to use, works well, and is free, but you can use paper or another medium to organize your process. To start, separate tasks into three columns: '"to-do", "in progress", and "done".

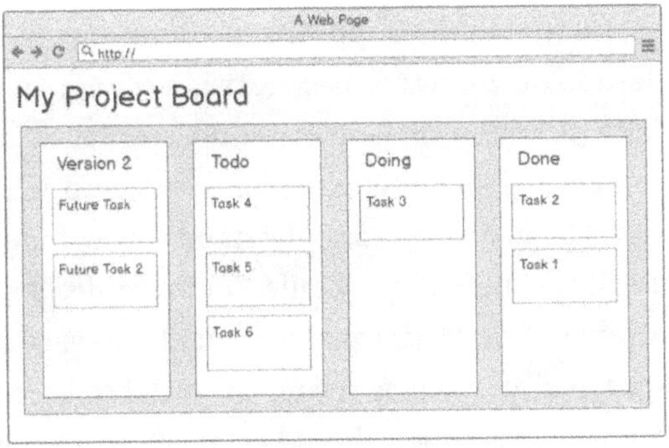

At first, your tasks can be a simple description detailing

what needs done. As your projects become more complex, you can use colors, tags, or more columns to separate your tasks into front-end, back-end, and other categories. Throughout your career, you will probably see many different styles of project management, from Kanban to Agile to Scrum. Every company does things a little differently, and it's important to not be too pedantic about the specifics and use whatever system is simple yet robust enough for the project at hand.

Any features not included in the MVP should go on a bucket list for future versions of the app. For example, when you finish the MVP, you can go on to version 2, then 3, and so on. If you want to keep lists of tasks that will go into future versions, you can add columns like "Version 2" or "Bucket List" or "Ideas", so long as they are separate from your MVP items.

Project Planning Steps:

1. Write down the ideas and goals for the application.
2. Create user stories. User stories are extremely useful for building apps that achieve your desired outcomes. A user story is a statement like "as a [user], I want [some ability] in order to [do something]." The statement answers who, what, and why in an easy to understand way without any implementation details. For example, "As a teacher, I want to be able to digitally manage my students' attendance records, in order to become more efficient." You should create at least a few of these statements for each type of user of your

application. Larger or more complex applications will have more.

3. Write down the list of requirements needed for the desired outcomes from the user stories, every piece of the app you need to build. These requirements should answer the question of "how" you will implement features. Go over that list and boil it down to make sure it is the minimum number of features actually required to build a working app. Remember your aim is an MVP.
4. Draw mockups for each of your screens— create schemas and diagrams for any database relationships; and map out your API (application programming interface - for back-end development) if you have one. Mockups can be as simple as using paper or a greaseboard to outline a rectangle with details inside for each screen; or using a software application made for this purpose (my favorite one that I've been using for many years is Balsamiq). You can use the same tools to diagram your schemas and database relationships, or you could use a specialized tool like dbdiagram.io which has a free tier for personal projects.
5. Based on your requirements, decide which features need built first and break that process down into steps, then create tasks based on those steps. Use a tool like Trello to enter all of your tasks and keep track of what you are working on and what you need to do next.

Having a process like the one I detail above will really

help you with not only building better applications (without missing important steps), but also with impressing employers with your organizational skills and attention to detail. Virtually every company is going to have a process with steps like these, and you'll be able to contribute to the team more effectively if you're familiar with this process or one like it.

I highly recommend watching the *Intro to Agile Crash Course* video on my YouTube channel, Faraday Academy, to learn more about software project management.

TIP: Tasks Should be Actionable

In the book *Getting Things Done* by David Allen, he recommends beginning all your tasks with an action word, like "walk the dog" or "wash the car.". This helps turn your vague statements into workable tasks and propels you to action as you are looking through your list. It's a best practice when creating your "to-do" list that you also make your tasks specific and measurable, even if you know beforehand that the end result will take a significant amount of time. Break down your larger goals and items into smaller tasks until they can be completed within a few hours, ideally. Keeping your tasks organized and actionable will come in handy in your first role, especially when you're working with a team.

There are many other pieces of great advice contained in the book *Getting Things Done* and I recommend you read it for yourself.

Finishing the Projects that you Start

> "Forcing yourself to just focus on one project at a time and not abandon it and switch to another one, that's the real important [part] of being able to finish projects."
>
> — Jared Wilcurt, interviewed on my podcast, Faraday Tech Cafe

Building projects can be fun, but also stressful. You will inevitably run into many hiccups during the process and feel frustrated when it gets difficult. Undoubtedly, the next shiny technology or language will come along and you'll want to build something new, putting off (sometimes forever) the current project you are working on. This road only leads to project graveyards and not having anything great to show for your work.

What is the solution? Make a list of all the projects you want to build and just work on one, or *maybe* two, at a time. Only start working on a new one when you have built a working MVP and are satisfied with the outcome, which can vary depending on the type of project.

Senior Software Engineer and prolific project creator, Jared Wilcurt, says that there are three types of projects you can build:

1. **Academic projects** where you are just trying to learn something new and do not care about the final result. This type of project is for educational purpose and can be thrown away after you finish learning what you need to. Most of your early projects will fit in this category.

2. **Portfolio projects** where you want to impress an employer. These are the projects where you use the technologies you are best at and really polish the end product. They should be well documented and adhere to best practices as much as possible.
3. **Passion projects** where you want something to exist so you build it yourself. This is the most difficult type of project and will likely take a long time to complete. You will probably have to put it aside to work on other things off and on so it does not consume all of your time.

When you decide what type of project you are working on, it becomes clearer what your end goal is and when to move on to the next project. You should build projects from end to end to get an idea for how the whole process works, and what difficulties or issues arise at various steps along the way.

See more tips for building projects on my podcast episode where I interview Jared: faradaytechcafe.podbean.com/e/episode-14-how-to-finish-projects-craft-resumes-with-the-jared-wilcurt

Project Advice

After you complete a project, you should host it somewhere on the internet. This not only helps you get used to hosting your code in a live environment (what programmers call "pushing your code to production") but it also lets you share your project and get feedback from others. There are many good options for free and easy hosting when you are starting out: Github Pages, Heroku, Digital Ocean, and others.

Challenge yourself to optimize the websites and applications you build. Ask yourself, "How can I make this better? Is there anything I can clean up in the code? Are there lines of code that are not being used anymore and need to be removed? What types of optimization would I be able to implement in a reasonable amount of time?" Asking yourself these questions is a great way to improve your skills. This also helps you prepare for interview questions about optimization.

As you are learning, do not forget that the foundational concepts in programming are immensely important. Many people make the mistake of learning tools and coding libraries without understanding the basic concepts first. This can be detrimental in the long run, making it harder to score well in technical interviews or to understand and fix bugs in your programs. While building applications, it is important to stay curious and always ask why something works the way it does. Sometimes you will not understand the answer right away - which is normal! Eventually, however, doing this will help you gain a deeper understanding of how the underlying technologies work.

You might also feel like you aren't progressing fast enough. Or maybe you cannot make the connection between what you are learning and practical use cases. This is also completely normal. There are a lot of pieces of information that you will need reviewed repeatedly, even after you get a job.

Conclusion

Take the learning plan from the previous chapter and start working your way through this curriculum. If you get stuck, just keep pushing through and reach out for help from the community when you need it. I've included a list of places to seek help in the the recommended resources for this book. The rest of this book will be a guide to help you land your first job as a programmer. Do not wait to finish reading it to start on the curriculum.

Action Steps:

1. Research job listings related to your goals and take notes on the keywords you find.
2. Look over some online curriculums and choose whether to use one of them or create your own.
3. Start studying and working on your first project within the first week if you can. Do not forget to plan appropriately before beginning to build an application.
4. Challenge yourself to optimize after every project.
5. Host projects online and ask other people to provide feedback.

7

HOW TO LEARN COMPUTER LANGUAGES

> "Everybody in this country should learn how to program a computer, because it teaches you how to think."
>
> — Steve Jobs, Visionary, Founder of Apple

Programming languages can be very intimidating, but one thing to understand is that human language is much more complex than any coding language. Computers are built to follow your instructions. You give them commands and they follow without inserting their own understanding or bias, and are based entirely on logic.

This chapter covers the basics of learning computer languages - from the fundamentals to becoming job-ready coders.

The Fundamentals

The first step to learning any programming language is the syntax. The fundamentals will always be similar: variables, operations, conditionals, and functions. This is an important stage because it will be the foundation for more advanced concepts later.

What are fundamentals? Here are some examples:

- Variables
- Data types
- Conditionals
- Operators
- Comments
- Functions
- Loops
- Scope
- User input
- Debugging
- Error handling
- APIs

When learning these concepts, do not pressure yourself to understand everything right away. If you see other students progressing faster or if it takes you a while for the concepts to click, that's okay! Absorb the information and keep searching for answers, and understanding will follow.

The most important thing is to correctly learn these fundamentals first. You can build some cool projects with many tools that people have built to help you write code faster, but if you do not fully understand the basics of programming, you are going to struggle to generalize and adapt your knowledge to new challenges you face.

Understanding the fundamentals of a computer language well will take you far in this career.

Tips for Starting

First, do not stick with one learning style if it is not working for you. Do not ever think, "I do not get it, I must not be smart enough." If you cannot understand a concept, then perhaps it is not being explained to you in the right way. Maybe you need a different instructor or a different medium. Make sure that your learning materials align with how you best absorb information. If you prefer books, then borrow or purchase a book. If you prefer video courses, then you can surf YouTube or go to one of the many sites with video courses (I recommended some earlier in the book) and find some great videos on any language or topic to put in your curriculum.

Second, do not pick large problems to solve right away. Before you tackle a large passion project, you need to throw away some projects and become comfortable coding in a sandbox before you get out into the real world of programming. This will help you assess your abilities and cultivate realistic expectations. More often than not, beginners quit if they set their expectations too high initially.

Build small tools and apps, then medium-sized tools and apps, all the while writing and reading plenty of code as you go. You should work on your passion projects last, helping you avoid the mistakes and headaches caused by unmet expectations.

While you are learning, you will likely encounter several online tutorials. Online tutorials and walkthroughs often do not bring up the bugs and issues that you might face. The coding process looks perfect when you are reading through a well-written article or watching an edited YouTube video; the person makes no mistakes and the project just goes smoothly. That is not reality. Usually bugs and issues are edited out and the senior developers who make those tutorials have spent years solving the bugs that you are going to deal with. If you are struggling to relate to a senior developer on YouTube, go watch some programming livestreams on Twitch or YouTube (especially mine!) and you will see plenty of mistakes with live debugging.

Do not forget that when you are following a tutorial, something that works in someone else's browser on their particular operating system might not work the same on your machine. There is a meme that says "Works on my computer" because this is such a common thing that happens. Programs work invariably in different environments sometimes. Do not get discouraged if a tutorial is not working correctly for you, just do the best you can and try to follow the problem solving steps I list later in this chapter.

Avoiding Outdated Information

When you are looking up information or coding resources online, make sure you check the date it was published and what versions of the technologies they are teaching. If the tutorial or resource is more than 3-4 years old (and sometimes even less than that) it is probably using an outdated version and it is better to look for something more up to date. Technology changes very quickly and you are bound to run into issues from using old code or material. The exception to this "date rule" is concepts. Software development and computer science concepts usually withstand the test of time, unlike specific technologies.

You should also check the versions of languages and libraries (tools) that you are using. In software, versions usually consist of three numbers separated by periods. For example, 1.2.8 or 3.0.24. Each number starts at zero and increments every time the code is updated. The type of coding changes will denote which of the three numbers increments. The first number is called the major version, where there will be a huge difference between versions, significantly decreasing the likelihood of full compatibility with previous versions. So, if you are looking at a library that is currently at version 4.0.2, then you should not look at any tutorials or resources that cover version 3.x.x or 2.x.x or 1.x.x, only 4.0.0 and above. However, if the library is version 3.5.5, then you can probably following along with a tutorial or use code from a Stack Overflow answer that is from version 3.1.0 because the major version is the same. *More on copying code from sites like Stack Overflow later on.*

It is the same with programming languages, too. Check out the latest major version for the language you are learning and try to stick to resources that cover that. If you are learning Python, make sure you are using the latest major version, Python 3, and not looking at outdated code from Python 2 or before. It is always good to start with the latest LTS (long-term support) or stable version if you can. For example, Python's latest stable version released is 3.9.0.

Solving Problems

Programming is not about the being able to type fast, be a genius, or know a lot about math – it is about problem solving. When you learn how to break down problems into individual steps and then solve each one according to best practices and recommended patterns, you will be ready to get your first job as a developer.

The Programmer Mindset

When you first start coding, work to develop a programmer mindset. We are taught in (most) schools to follow instructions, but when you are learning to code, you must throw that notion out the window. The best way to learn to code is to break things, to ask yourself, "What if ...?" often.

Treat the language like a playground. Try changing things and see what happens. It is important to not just follow code-along tutorials but to break out of what the tutorial is doing. The students I have seen who adopted a programmer mindset early on and continued to ask "why", did much better overall than their peers. This is something you have to consciously work on, it is a mindset change!

Here are some ways to start practicing this: When you are following a tutorial or building a project, comment things out, move things around, change variable names, rearrange files. Do anything to break out of that mindset of following steps in order. Did you get an error? Did the program run differently at all? Take note of what happens when you make changes.

You are capable of doing this! Start practicing now.

Thinking in Logic

Daniel Lomelino, a senior instructor at the Kenzie Academy coding school, says, "One of the biggest problems that students have is not understanding the problem. They jump into the code right away and get stuck on small implementation details and forget about what they are trying to solve." He says that he always tries to help students see the bigger picture and then break things down into steps. It is important to figure out "how" to do something before deciding on "what" to do.

Here are the problem solving steps that he recommends following:

1. First, try to understand the problem and figure out how you can best do that. It might be writing out the problem in your own words or pretending to explain the problem out loud to someone (this is known as *rubber ducking* in the programming world).
2. Break the problem up into small, manageable steps.
3. Write pseudocode for the logical steps. *Pseudocode is typically a series of comments in your code (or words on a paper or a greaseboard) that describe what the code might do without writing real code yet. It is quite useful for quickly stepping through problems.*
4. Then try to solve the problem step by step.

If you have already gone through these steps and you are really stuck on something, start over. Save your current code somewhere or comment it out and re-write the whole program or file from scratch. Sometimes this "nuclear option" technique catches less obvious errors that you made.

Practice these steps with problem solving and find the techniques that work best for you. Then, share them with me!

Debugging

Bugs are issues or mistakes in your code that can cause your programs to stop running ("crash") or behave in a way that you did not intend. Sometimes bugs are obvious to detect, such as when you misspell a word or forget a semicolon that causes your program not to run correctly. Sometimes they are not as obvious, like when you are trying to import someone else's library into your program and it does not work as expected.

Debugging (the act of attempting to fix bugs) is a good opportunity to see where you need to improve and to practice your problem solving skills. There are courses that teach debugging skills which can be helpful, but for the most part, you must pick up these skills through deliberate practice. Running into difficult bugs is one of the most challenging parts of programming and, unfortunately, it discourages many beginners .

I talked about needing a mindset shift a little earlier in this chapter regarding thinking like a programmer. A change of mindset is also needed for debugging. When you see error messages or your program is not working correctly, becoming upset or frustrated is not helpful. Instead, appreciate those moments because they make you grow the most as a programmer. If you never ran into difficulties, you would have no opportunities to practice problem solving skills, which you must master and continually improve to be a successful programmer.

Error messages are there to help you. Next time you see an error, really take your time to read it line by line. Most of the time, somewhere in the error message, you will see file and variable names that you recognize. Look at where those error messages are pointing to. Usually it will give you a filename with a line number of where the problem happened in your code. From there, you can try commenting out lines of code to isolate the problem. You will also probably have to print out the value of variables (and the type of the variable if you are using a language like JavaScript or Python). You can fix the most common bugs with these steps.

If you still cannot figure out how to solve the bug, try copying your error message (remove any specific variable or file names) and pasting the error text into an online search engine. You will probably see that other people have asked about this error before on sites like Stack Overflow or in a Github issues section. Sometimes you can quickly see the answer to your problem and other times, you will see many people offering up different solutions. In the latter case, you should read through all possible solutions and their explanations before choosing one because you will not have the experience to discern which solution is the best by just looking at the code. This will come with time and practice.

TIP: SHOULD YOU COPY CODE?

"Code monkey" is sometimes used as a derogatory term for developers who just copy code, but it is not always bad to copy. No one can remember every bit of syntax and all of us use bits and pieces of each other's code in one way or another.

Copying has a negative connotation because sometimes people copy snippets of code without understanding how they work. Random pieces of code strung together like this can lead to a very unstable codebase. Make sure you understand what the code is doing before you paste it into your program. Copying is a shortcut, not a replacement for understanding. In the beginning, do the extra research to know what the pros and cons might be for the block of code that you want to copy. If it is using a "reduce" method, for example, and you have not encountered that before, you should look it up and try out an example first.

Copying is used when you need a solution to an acute problem or you do not remember the exact syntax that you need to use, and if you encounter some methods or terms you have not seen before, take the time to do some research instead of blindly pasting into your code and expecting it to run. When you are experienced, you will be able to look at a block of code and know what it is doing and be able to quickly determine whether to use it or not, or at least where to find more information.

Leveling Up

You need some level of hand-holding at the beginning for direction, but do not get too comfortable. While you are learning, you are also working toward becoming a software craftsman, a professional trying to create the only the highest quality software.

You can reach that next level by practicing your problem solving and debugging skills.. Here are some more tips I have for you based on my experience (many of these are mentioned elsewhere in the book and are just being compiled together here):

- **Always Try to Think in Terms of Challenges, not Annoyances**
- **Learn Programming Patterns and Paradigms**
- **Learn Algorithms**
- **Learn Computer Science**
- **Learn How to Write Tests for Your Code:** People

often neglect writing tests to make sure their code is working properly. They just assume that it is fine (and will stay fine) and move on to writing more code, making the long-term maintenance of the software much more difficult. Testing is important because helps you write better code, that is easier to maintain and it impresses companies. In fact, learning how to write tests might make you stand out as a developer more than anything else because so few software developers can write tests.

- **Practice Reading Documentation:** Every language or tool you will use will have some information and instructions for its use on a website. This is what we call documentation, or docs for short. You will hear many people say, "read the docs," or things like, "you do not need any other resources, just look at the docs." To a beginner, documentation can be somewhat confusing, so it's better to use a resource, like one of the courses or curriculums I mentioned in previous chapters until you become more comfortable with the coding terminology. However, as you level up past the basics and gain more understanding about programming, it is important to learn how to read and understand documentation on your own. These docs can be intimidating at first, but just start reading them without pressuring yourself to understand everything. Soon you will be able to understand and navigate documentation, which will help take you to the next level with your coding.
- **Read Lots of Other People's Code**

- **Practice Reading Source Code**
- **Learn Some Digital Security Basics:** It is vital to understand that any code that we write and deploy somewhere could be vulnerable to malicious actors trying to steal data or intellectual property. This could include SQL Injection, cross-site scripting, man-in-the-middle attacks, etc. I recommend learning from security professional, Nathan House. He is very experienced in the industry and is a great teacher with courses on Udemy and his own website, stationx.net. I have learned a lot from his courses.
- **Read Books About Concepts and Techniques:** For example, *Clean Code* by Robert C. Martin and, *The Pragmatic Programmer* by Andrew Hunt and David Thomas.
- **Watch Conference Talks:** Find ones that cover topics in your field of study and about software development in general. A lot of these are free on YouTube.
- **Maintain Code Quality:** Take care of yourself and always double check any code that you wrote when you were tired or feeling stressed. Here is a Twitter thread about the topic that I found to be very insightful: twitter.com/hillelogram/status/1119709859979714560.

Conclusion

Learning to code can feel like an emotional roller coaster – one moment it can be scary, intimidating, and overwhelming and the next it is exciting or exhilarating. You need to mentally prepare yourself for the challenges coding can bring, and try not to sweat the small things.

I highly recommend you check out the talk, How to Think Like a Programmer, by Andy Harris (it is on YouTube). He is a developer from my local Python user's group and was a huge inspiration for me writing this chapter. In the video, he goes into more detail about some of the things that I talk about in this chapter.

Action Steps:

1. Spend a lot of time getting good at the fundamentals and really understanding them.
2. Practice your problem solving skills as much as possible.
3. Always strive to level up as a software craftsman.

8

OPEN SOURCE PROJECTS

> "In open source, we feel strongly that to really do something well, you have to get a lot of people involved."
>
> — Linus Torvalds, Creator of Linux

Working on your own projects for a portfolio or even pairing up with another learner is great, but there are skills you won't learn until you work with other developers in real-world projects. How do you get real-world experience while you are still learning? By contributing to open source software.

Open source is defined by Wikipedia as, "a product [that] includes permission to use its source code, design documents, or content. It most commonly refers to the open-source model, in which open-source software... released under an open-source license as part of the open-source-software movement." In an open source environment, developers upload their code and let other programmers see, update, and use it (usually) for free.

These other programmers will probably use different

tools and employ different writing styles than you, and you will have to learn the different standards for merging your code into theirs. You will learn about testing, deployments, and versioning your work, all of which push you to learn and grow much more quickly than you would on your own.

Open source code usually lives in repositories, or "repos" on sites like github.com. Since Github is the most common place to host these repositories, you will become intimately familiar with it as you progress on your coding journey. You are going to be interacting with open source tools and software made by other technologists every day as you are learning and throughout your career. This chapter will guide you through the process of finding and contributing to open source projects.

Finding Beginner-friendly Projects

It can be daunting to contribute to another person's project for the first time. Thinking that you are not qualified and less capable than others is a common setback for beginners. It is also hard to go from reading and understanding code that you wrote yourself to something another person wrote.

You can start off very small by making simple updates to documentation files - the files that explain how some piece of software works to humans - or by creating a text tutorial for a particular piece of software and submitting it to the people who maintain that software. If you speak multiple languages, you can also offer to translate text in an open source web or mobile app. This will help you get used to the process and you can work your way up from there.

Many communities around open source projects have implemented methods to welcome new developers who want to contribute. If you look at any repository on Github

(Scout App for example), there will be an "issues" tab at the top. Click on that and you will see a list of problems with the software (bugs), questions from users, requests for additional functionality, and more. Most projects will separate all of these different issues with "tags" so you can easily tell them apart when scrolling through or searching for them. Tags are all of the colorful words next to the issue's title:

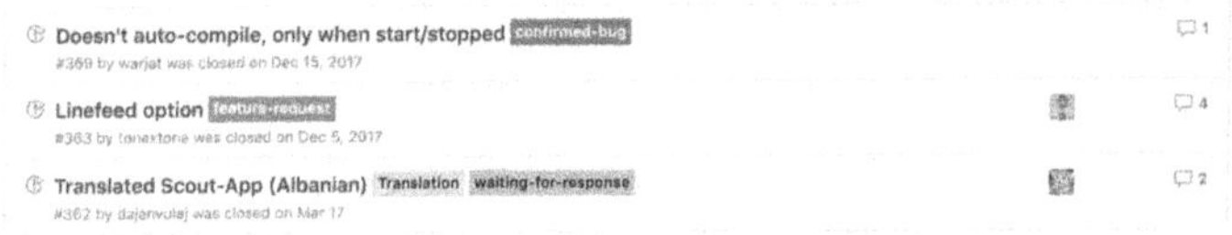

Most of the time, the coders who own and maintain one of these repositories will be more than happy to let you contribute and may even help walk you through the process. A good place to start is by looking for issues that are tagged something like "help wanted" or "good first issue".

Here are some places that I highly recommend when starting out:

Repo Name	Tags	Details
Vue.js	good first issue, contribution welcome	Vue.js is a JavaScript library that's well known for its focus on being welcoming to newcomers
freeCodeCamp	first timers welcome, language: ..., hacktoberfest	freeCodeCamp is an organization whose mission is to help people learning to code - including making their first contribution

Pick an issue on the list, click on it and scroll down through the comments. If you understand what the problem is and no one has posted that they are actively working on it, you can make a comment saying you would like to try. This could mean testing out the problem to see if it is really a bug or updating the actual code. If you do not understand the problem fully, feel free to post a comment asking for clarification.

You will use a plethora of libraries in your personal

projects as you are learning to code. Soon you will realize that none of them are perfect! There will be plenty of quirks, bugs, and misspellings. Why not volunteer to fix the problems that you find since someone else built the software for you to use for free? You won't always be able to fix the problem, but it doesn't hurt to create an issue about it and try to find a solution. If you do not spot any problems yourself, you can always search through the issues in these libraries as well.

The examples I list above are just related to JavaScript. Here is a more comprehensive list of other projects that are friendly towards beginners as well: awesome-for-beginners. More recommendations for contributing are listed on my website: gwenfaraday.com/learn-to-code-book.

How to make your first contribution

Contributing to open source projects has several steps involved, as well as some new terminology. Fortunately, this process has been fairly standardized. Here, I'm going to describe the process you can use for updating documentation or language translations. To perform more complicated contributions, you will have to learn a tool called Git and how to pull and run the code locally on your machine; then make changes and push it back up to Github and request to merge your changes into the repo.

The easiest way to get started is to contribute to your own project! You make your own repo on Github, then merge in changes that you make yourself. This will get you used to the process and make it less intimidating when you want to make changes to other peoples' projects.

First, signup at Github.com if you do not have an account already.

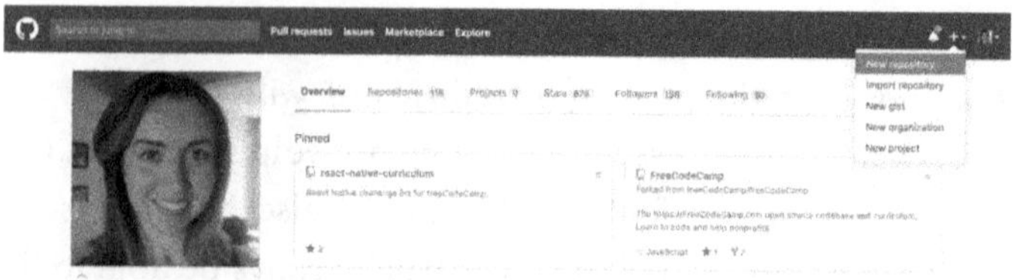

Second, click the plus button in the top right-hand corner and then select "New Repository".

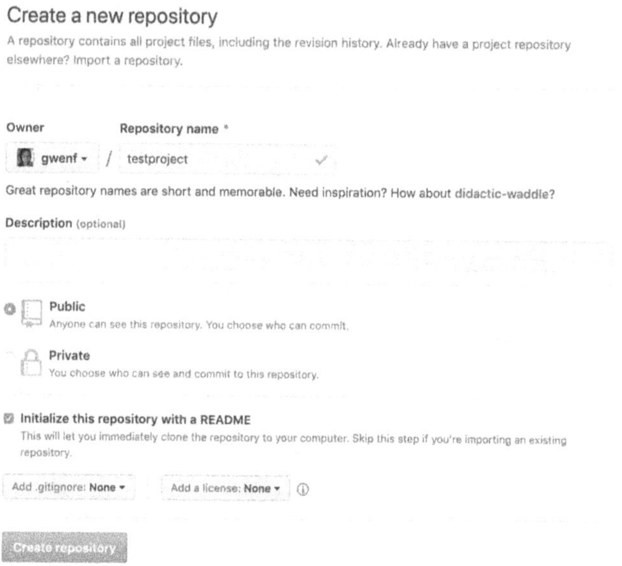

Give your project a name (you can update or delete it later). Make sure you select "Initialize this repository with a README" so you have a file to edit later. Then, click "Create Repository".

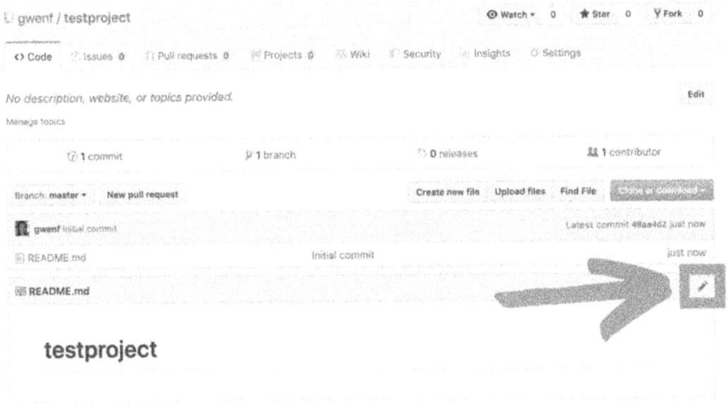

Notice that there is already one file there by default called README.md (because you told Github to create it when you set up the repo). This is a standard file found in most repos that describes important details about the project such as where to find help, how to download, install, and use the code, and steps or rules for contributing. When you first go to any repository, the styled output of the README.md file displays after the list of files, it is the first thing a visitor will see about a project. The ".md" at the end of the filename stands for Markdown, which is a markup language like HTML, but for formatting text. You can make headers, paragraphs, lists, and many other elements that you would create in a word processor, except you are doing it with code. I won't get into too many details here, but I have some links for learning markdown over at my book resources page. Markdown is easy to learn and it is good to know the basics. To edit the README.md file, click on the pencil icon in the upper right corner of the README.

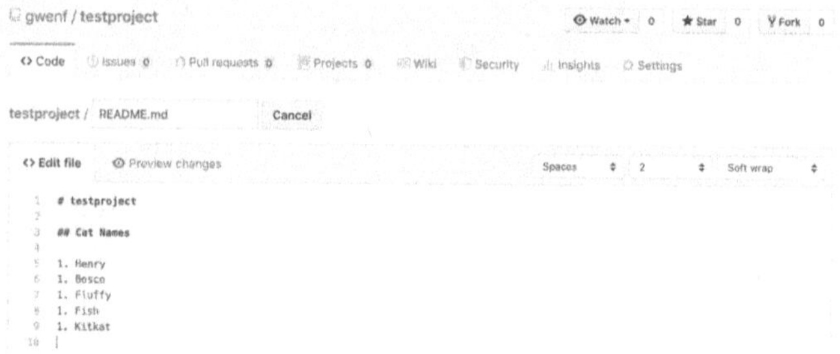

Now, let's add some markdown to the file. I'm adding a subheader here using `##` and then a list after it. Since everything has to be typed out in markdown, it would be really annoying if you had to renumber a list every time you wanted to move around or delete an item. Fortunately, Markdown lets you just use the number 1 for every list item and then it will number them correctly when it renders the styled page.

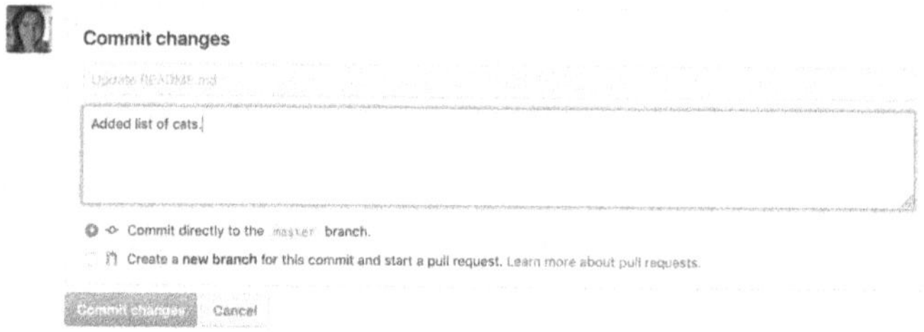

After you make your changes, you can scroll down the page to the "commit changes" box and enter a description of the changes you made - this is known as a "commit message". You will be writing a lot of these over the coming months and years. In the future you will be creating a new branch and requesting to merge it in with the current code by making a "pull request". It is fine to leave the option

"Commit directly to the master branch" for now though. Press the "commit changes" button and you are done!

You just made your first contribution! That's the same general process you will have to use when contributing to any repository, but it is missing one step. When you created the codebase on Github, you have all of the rights to update it. When someone else owns the repo, you can't just update it without their permission. That's where pull requests come in. A pull request (PR) is when someone wants to merge their code changes into the original repository, but needs permission. The changes must be made first, and then the request is made to update the original which gives the owner and other community members time to review, comment on, or request changes to the new code. Github lets you do this from its website. You click on the edit icon and it will show you the same interface as before, only with a message like this at the top:

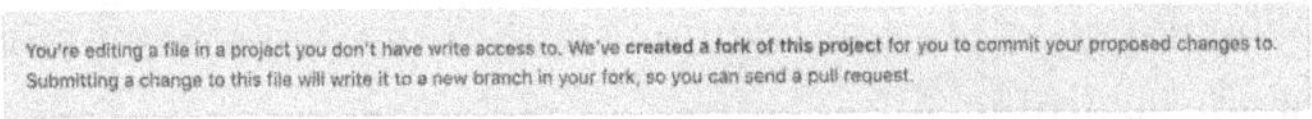

You're editing a file in a project you don't have write access to. We've created a fork of this project for you to commit your proposed changes to.
Submitting a change to this file will write it to a new branch in your fork, so you can send a pull request.

You do not have to understand what branches and forks mean yet. That will come when you start learning Git. Make your changes, scroll to the bottom, and write a commit message detailing the changes you made. The wording will ask you to propose file changes this time:

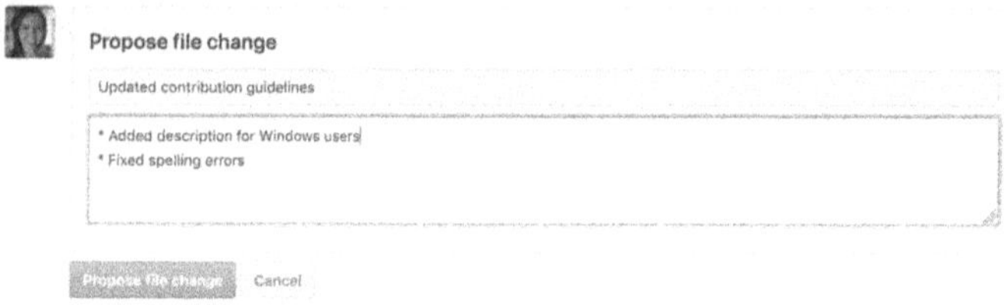

Clicking the "propose changes" button will automatically create a PR for you that you can view in the "Pull Requests" tab on the Github repo. Since the coders who work on these projects are almost always doing it for free, give them some time to get to your request. If they haven't responded in a week or two, you can post a comment on your PR tagging them (using @their_username) to remind them to take a look. Sometimes it takes a while or they might not end up merging your changes. Do not worry if that happens. It is a great learning experience whether or not your changes get accepted.

Conclusion

The term "open source" in this context is referring to community-driven tools where anyone can read through the code and attempt to contribute and make the project better. There are a great number of these projects, and you should be making simple contributions within the first few months of your learning.

Contributing to open source is a great idea for the following reasons:

- It teaches you know how to use version control (Git – you will learn this in your studies).
- You learn how to work on projects with other people.
- It teaches the important skills of updating and enhancing codebases that you did not create. These are things you will spend a lot of time doing as a professional!
- You are giving back to a community from which you benefit so much. As a programmer, you will be using free resources to learn and get help all the time. It is important to give back as well. This makes you look good *and* feel good.

Action Steps:

1. Select an open source project and start reading through the issues.
2. Take note of any bugs or feature requests, especially if they are tagged as "easy", "documentation", "translation", "first-timer", or similar.
3. Make the requested changes to the code.
4. Create a PR.
5. Add a link to the PR you created in the original issue. It is a good idea to link the original issue in the PR description as well.
6. Check up on the PR to see if anyone has commented on it.

9

PAIR PROGRAMMING

"Employers not only recognize, but increasingly more often *expect* to see collaborative work on individual portfolios... This is quite simply because very few work individually in production, and nobody works without having to communicate on the job."

— Julius Dobos, Cogswell Polytechnical College

Collaboration skills are worth their weight in gold. As a professional, you will almost certainly work with other developers, designers, and businesspeople on every project, almost every day. A great way to learn these skills and improve your ability to communicate is through pair programming.

Pair programming involves two people meeting together in person or online to share a screen and work on something together. This might include working on a project, building a quick demo, or completing a challenge on a site like freeCodeCamp. Depending on the setup, you might have two keyboards, mouses, and mirrored monitors connected to the same computer. This works well if you are pairing in person, although you could just as easily have one person observing while the other person controls the keyboard and mouse. Another way to partition responsibilities is to have screen sharing programs that virtually connect both users' computers and allow them to simultaneously write and edit code without having to take turns.

This chapter details how to find a partner and get started with pair programming.

Benefits of Pair Programming

Here is a quick list of the common benefits of pair programming while you are learning and looking for your first job. Many employers use pair programming on the job to help with on-boarding, training, and solving certain problems in the code (sometimes two heads are better than one!).

- Get help for problems you are struggling with
- Receive support and encouragement
- Learn faster through teaching and observing
- Good for interview preparation
- Write better code
- Validate your ideas and solutions
- Opportunity to build relationships

Finding a Partner

You have a few options to find a partner for pair programming. The first is going to local meetups or tech events and asking the people you meet if they would like to pair with you. Working together in person is great for building personal connections and helps with improving communication skills. In my experience, it is also a good way to find someone with more experience than you who is willing to mentor you as well as pair program.

A second option is to post on a coding forum or chatroom that you are looking for a pair programming partner. This is the easiest way to find a peer at a similar level as you and enable the two of you to push each other to grow. Some good websites for finding a partner are the freeCodeCamp forum and Code Newbies chatroom or Facebook groups. You can also try the "programming" and "learnprogramming" subreddits (forums on Reddit.com); they both have large, active communities. *Note: There are websites like CodeMentor.com that allow you to pay to pair program and receive coaching from senior software developers. If you feel like you need a mentor and cannot find one locally, it might be a good option.*

Getting Started

Start by collectively choosing a project or problem to work on. If it is your first time with a partner, it is best to select a programming exercise that can be completed within a few hours. freeCodeCamp or Hackerrank (hackerrank.com) challenges are perfect for this. You can also try to build small features like a menu or shopping page directly in Glitch.com, Codepen.io, or JSFiddle.net so there is no time lost from having to set things up locally. This will let you see how well you work together and, if there is a connection, you can pair on some more complex problems or applications in the future.

How to Screen Share

Fortunately, there are many free platforms available for screen sharing. If you do not have a solution already, I recommend checking out these options: Glitch, Visual Studio Code, Zoom, Skype, and Discord.

As of the writing of this book, Glitch is my favorite option to virtually collaborate with others on small projects. It allows you to work in the same virtual codebase and add, edit, save, and display HTML, CSS, and JavaScript files. They even have an option for building a back-end with Node.js in their browser-based interface. The only catch is that there isn't a voice chat yet so you will probably want to use Skype or another platform to make a voice call and then work on the code inside Glitch.com.

Zoom, Discord, and Skype all have similar functionality. They let one participant share their screen with the other people on the call. I have used all three of these and they work well for collaborating. Discord is a bit more finicky than the other two because you have to be "friends" and start a private chat to use video calling and screen sharing features. Zoom limits you to calls that last 50 minutes for the free plan, so it might not be the best option for longer calls.

Visual Studio Code is a great free code editor that has a live sharing feature for screen sharing and working in the same codebase simultaneously. This option works well for any size of project. There is also an extra plugin that allows you to make a voice call directly from the VS Code interface (Live Share Audio plugin).

You can also use virtual desktop software or other tools, as long as they do not take too long to set up. The tools I list above are battle-tested, simple, and free to use. They also work on all major operating systems: Linux, Mac, and Windows.

Since available screen sharing options seem to change frequently, please check my website for current recommendations: gwenfaraday.com/learn-to-code-book.

~

TIP: What to do about Imposter Syndrome

Imposter Syndrome is term you will encounter many times as you are learning to code. What exactly is it and why is it relevant?

Wikipedia defines Imposter Syndrome as "a psychological pattern in which an individual doubts their accomplishments and... despite external evidence of their competence, those experiencing this phenomenon remain convinced that they are frauds, and do not deserve all they have achieved." In other words, it means that you see other people around you as being more intelligent or as better programmers while downplaying your own abilities. While it is completely normal to feel inexperienced when you are learning something new, impostor syndrome involves an inferiority complex where you "incorrectly attribute [your] success to luck, or as a result of deceiving others into thinking [you] are more intelligent than [you] perceive [yourself] to be (Wikipedia)."

This complex can come up at any stage of your learning: while you are just starting out with pair programming, giving a technical talk, or even years down the road in your career. It also happens to nearly everyone when they start a new job. When you're new to a role, it is easy to view the people who are already working at a company as smarter or more advanced than you just because they have had time to learn the tech stack ahead of you. Everyone needs ramp up time at a new company or on a new project, and anyone who shames you for not understanding or asking questions is out of touch.

When you experience these feelings, try to catch yourself and remember how far you have come in your journey. Think about all of your accomplishments— all of the coding challenges you completed or apps you built. Many people desire to learn but never start. You are already ahead of them because you are reading this book and taking the first steps to becoming a software engineer. That is something you should be proud of!

Remember what Bob Ross said: "Talent is just a pursued interest." Anyone that you perceive to be more talented than you now has had the opportunity to pursue and perfect their programming skills longer than you have up to this point. You can get there if you continue to push yourself.

Conclusion

Pair programming is a very useful practice while you are learning to code. Start pair programming as early as possible - within your first month or two - and set a goal to do it on a regular basis.

Action Steps:

1. Find a partner.
2. Schedule a pair programming session.

3. Reflect on how to make it better in the future.
4. Set a recurring date to do it every week or two if you can.
5. Repeat: Stick with the same partner or find a new one!

10

HACKATHONS

What is a hackathon? It actually has nothing to do with the nefarious "hacking" you see in movies. It is an event where a bunch of people get together, form groups, and try to build something within a certain amount of time (usually 24-48 hours). I've been to, and have run, quite a few hackathons over the last four years and I would like to share some of what I have learned and make an argument here for why attending these types of events might be beneficial to you.

Every time I attend a hackathon, it feels like I am getting a month's worth of learning, all crammed into a day or two. Yes, it can be long and tiring but the experience can pay dividends. On top of that, I've connected with some amazing people, built some cool projects (most of my portfolio outside of work), and incorporated a company. All of this has really helped to boost my career as a programmer.

Types of Hackathons

There are many different types of hackathons, but they all have several things in common:

- **Time limit**: usually between 24 and 48 hours
- **Theme**: organizers will ask that you build a certain type of application (like Internet-of-Things) or they'll tell you to use a certain technology
- **Prizes**: generally awarded for the best overall applications and for apps that fit into certain categories or use a certain technology

In most cases, there is plenty of information online about the rules, judging, technologies, etc. It doesn't take long to read about the event and avoid surprises when you get there. Quite a few hackathons are only for college students, and in those cases adults can sometimes attend as mentors, but not participants.

Several hackathons I have been to have even had a Q&A or panel discussion at the beginning to talk about what they were looking for in app submissions. Some also have online boards so you can team up and get to know other participants prior to the event. Meeting staff and participants early on can help ease any social anxiety and give you a confidence boost.

Why should you go?

I already mentioned some reasons but here is an overview:

1. **Networking**: This is a given. I've met politicians, business people, developers, designers, and plenty of rockstars (figuratively, of course 😊) at these events. I'm shy, but I force myself to get out and meet at least a few people each time. I've never regretted meeting someone at a hack!
2. **Portfolio**: I have several solid, well-designed portfolio pieces that came out of hackathons. Some companies have talked to me because they liked what I built at one. Make sure you get on a team where you think you will fit in well and try to work on an idea you are passionate about, or at least very interested in. Having a designer on the team is super helpful, but I always try to look at some design inspiration before I go so I can whip up a layout and design doc if necessary. I think it is good to treat every project as a potential portfolio app.
3. **Confidence**: I have found it surprisingly common that new developers think their skills are sub-par and that they will not be able to make meaningful contributions to a team. Plenty of non-technical people are needed at these events and even people who want to code but only know HTML or CSS can help on a team.
4. **Teamwork**: The importance of learning to work with other developers when you are new cannot be overstated. You learn to partition tasks, share a codebase, and get along in a stressful environment. Sometimes apps crash and things do not work out, or you or your teammate will feel tired or frustrated by the end of it. Going

through this experience together forces you to learn how to work together through the good and the bad as a team.

5. **Communication Skills**: As a good teammate, you should always be talking to your group. "I just pushed code, can you pull." "I'm working on this..." "How are you doing with that?" "You seem frustrated, let's take a walk and get some fresh air." It forces you be open and explicit about what you are thinking and doing. More importantly, it makes you think about what's going on around you and how your teammates are doing. Your communication skills will improve!
6. **Learning New Tech Skills**: It is hard to set aside time to constantly improve your skills and start dreaming up and building new applications. You will most likely be forced to use technologies that you have never used before: because your team will bring different skills and levels of experience to the table, and because the project you end up working on will probably require you to try something new.
7. **Experience the Lifecycle of a Project:** You will generally be planning, designing, building, and iterating on your app to achieve an MVP (minimum viable product). This can give you a glimpse of what the whole software development cycle will look like on a small scale. Going through this process can give you a head start - and a boost of confidence - at your first job.

What to expect

Expect the unexpected. Things will go wrong with your code. Venues will be overly loud or surprisingly cold. You may need to pivot on your idea after you have already started working on it. Whatever the source of stress is, remember to take a deep breath and stay flexible.

The best thing you can do is to prepare as much as you can. Most hackathons (if they are 24+ hours) expect some participants stay overnight and they will have some couches to crash on. Even if I live close, I usually do not end up going home to sleep because I know I will sleep longer than intended. If you do want to go home for the night or just need a break, do not feel pressured into staying just because the rest of your team is. You have to take care of your needs first.

In preparation for staying up very late (or overnight) it is not a bad idea to bring extra warm clothes, a blanket and pillow (or, better, a sleeping bag), snacks, and energy beverages (most hackathons will supply sodas, energy drinks, coffee, and snacks - just make sure to find out before you go). Before you leave your house, check and make sure you have extra headphones, chargers, and all the devices you are going to need as well as daily items that you use. With a little planning, I am much more productive and end up having more fun (and getting more sleep!).

To prepare for the technical aspects of the event, make sure you have read the rules and know what technologies are required and/or allowed. If you are new to coding, do not worry too much about knowing everything and do not feel like you are underqualified to attend. Teams need many different skillsets beyond just writing code - e.g. ideation, business and marketing, research, public speaking, and design, just to name a few.

If you want to overprepare for the coding part, knowing how to use generators or starter-kits can be a huge advantage going in. Sometimes it can take a long time to set up an application's codebase and using these kinds of shortcuts can prevent a lot of headaches and wasted time. It also allows you to do more actual coding without beating your head against a wall getting things set up from scratch. The less complicated your code is, the better: time is at a premium during these events and other people of various skill levels will likely be jumping in and coding with you. Plain old HTML, CSS, and JavaScript files are just fine. As long as your app works, everything else can be improved upon later.

Forego anything that isn't important to demoing the core functionality of your app. Login screens, cool animations, about pages; they can all be added later on if you decide to keep working on the project post-hackathon.

A note about building mobile apps: If you want to do an ambitious mobile app, that's great—as long as you are considering the time that it takes to set up Android Studio or Xcode and get all of the emulators up and running or devices working on whatever wifi they might have at that venue. I've done web, mobile, IoT, and cloud projects at hackathons and web apps are by far the fastest for me to set up and start building. If you do want to build a mobile app, it is probably best to use something that can run in a browser (like Cordova) so everyone on the team can easily contribute.

Finding the Right Hackathon

The best hackathons in my experience are civic and community-minded ones. If you live in the United States, many states host these types of events to try to come up with solutions to local problems like poverty, pollution, or nutrition. It is amazing to see random people come together and passionately work on something that could change lives. There are other hackathons that are sponsored by companies or organizations, and, like many sponsored events, may have a financial interest. Make sure if you go to one of those that you have done your research about the event and know for certain that your team will own the rights to what you worked on or be compensated appropriately for it.

Some of my favorite hackathons are Give Camp, Start-up Weekend, and Civic-minded local hacks. Most of these are free, or have a small fee to cover the costs of food and supplies. For more hackathon ideas, please see the resources for this book at gwenfaraday.com/learn-to-code-book.

Conclusion

If you can work it into your schedule, it is definitely worth it to attend a hackathon. Remember not to stress about perfection, it is all about learning and creating, with some friendly competition on the side.

Action Steps:

1. Research and sign up for a hackathon.
2. Attend the hackathon.

3. Write about your experience. Be sure to let me know by tweeting @faradayacademy.

11

STAYING CURRENT

"The core skill of a software engineer is being able to adapt to new technologies well; not just knowing one language or another."

— David M Gregg, Director of Software Eng. at Kenzie Academy

No matter what your path into coding is - whether you go through a bootcamp or choose to self-study - you will end up teaching yourself new things all the time. Technology is consistently moving forward, and, if you do not keep up on current trends, you can get left behind very quickly. If you get hired using one JavaScript framework now, you will probably need to learn another one within a few years, not to mention other tools that change every few months. If you learned all the best practices for programming last year, some of them might have already changed this year.

Many people are intimidated by this state of perpetual innovation, but if you keep up with every minute change, you won't get anything else done. Along your coding journey, you will find several tempting rabbit holes everywhere that are waiting to suck you in and waste your time. This is where having a plan comes into play.

Tools to Use

Some tools that are very helpful to stay in the loop with programming are podcasts, mailing lists, and micro-blogging platforms like Twitter. All three of these help you keep up to date in different ways (although the latter can be much more addictive and unproductive if not managed well).

Podcasts

There are many podcasts that sift through a lot of current and helpful information so you do not have to. They are also easy to listen to in the car during your commute, or while you are working out or cleaning. The idea is to let them supplement your studies with terms, ideas, and concepts.

Here are some useful podcasts to get started with:

- freeCodeCamp: Excellent quality, short, and to the point
- Code Newbie: Great podcast for new coders
- Learn to Code with Me: Self-taught programmer Laurence Bradford interviews guests about interesting topics (I was interviewed on this episode)
- Faraday Tech Cafe: This is my own podcast about software development
- Check out my list of favorite podcasts and

podcast apps at gwenfaraday.com/learn-to-code-book

Since there are so many different ones to subscribe to, it is a good idea to make lists of episodes you want to listen to during your weekly planning sessions. I like to use listennotes.com to search for podcasts, episodes, and topics; and compile those into lists that I can import into other podcast apps (make sure you are copying the RSS feed link).

Mailing Lists

Thousands of development articles are published everyday and it can take a lot of energy to sift through every single one of them for relevant information. Wouldn't it be so much easier to have someone else just send you curated lists of articles, videos, and other resources regularly?

Fortunately, for all of us, there are quite a few daily, weekly, and monthly email lists that do just that. Here are some examples (there are also plenty of other ones for every language or technology you can think of):

- Faraday Academy Weekly Newsletter - My weekly newsletter at my blog
- freeCodeCamp Newsletter - Sign up for an account on freecodecamp.org and make sure you have the "Send me Quincy's weekly email" setting turned on. Here is an archive of previous emails: freecodecamp.org/news/i-email-1-2-million-people-every-week-heres-what-i-say-to-them-3c62e6d9812a
- For more, see my list of developer newsletters: gwenfaraday.com/learn-to-code-book

Micro-blogging Platforms (e.g. Twitter)

A quick scroll through Twitter every few days can keep you reasonably up to date on the current happenings in tech. Set a rule to not spend more than 10 or 15 minutes on Twitter and then use a browser plugin to block social media, if necessary, to keep from overdoing it. Many people get caught up scrolling through feeds for extended amounts of time and it is not nearly as useful as spending that time working on your studies. I block all social media from my browser so I have to explicitly unblock it so it does not distract me from my work.

Here are some relevant tech influencers to follow for the latest tech info:

- Traversy Media - @traversymedia
- Quincy Larson - @ossia
- freeCodeCamp - @freeCodeCamp
- CodeNewbie - @CodeNewbies
- MDN Web Docs - @MozDevNet
- For a more comprehensive list of people and organizations to follow, please see: gwenfaraday.com/learn-to-code-book

This list is just for getting you started. As you meet people at events and grow a network, you will find many more people and groups to follow.

News Platforms

This has been my favorite way to consume tech news for the past year or so. Partly because these sites can have great new content every week, but also because they do not have the rest of the distractions of a regular social media type of site. I can just go to the site, read the news and leave without feeling tempted to do anything else. Here are my two favorite sites:

- **Tech Crunch:** They have a good search field so you can try searching for different types of content if you do not want to just scroll through the latest general news. There is no filtering though, so you may have to play around with searching for different terms until you're comfortable using it.
- **Hashnode and Dev.to:** These are some of my favorite places to scroll through and pick up new tidbits of information. They are developer-focused blogging platforms, so not technically news platforms, but with so many different writers, I find lots of information about new technologies that I had not heard about before.
- **Reddit:** You can check out some subreddit feeds like r/softwaredevelopment, r/development, and r/learnprogramming to get some fast updates on the world of technology. I do not go here that much anymore, but some of my developer friends use Reddit as their primary source of news information. So, check it out and see if you like it.

To-Read-Later Lists (e.g. Pocket)

What do you do when you find something you want to read, but do not have time right now? You should be keeping a bucket list for these items somewhere. I personally recommend using Pocket (getpocket.com) for this. It gives you an icon in the search bar at the top of your browser that lets you add items to your list with one click. You can also easily tag items as you add them to create separate lists by category.

Face-to-Face Meetings

Meeting and talking in person with other humans is sometimes underrated in this industry since you can get all your information online (and do your job entirely online, for that matter). Please do not underestimate the value of good old-fashioned communication. Attending meetups and study groups is a great way to get exposure, interviews, and recommendations, as well as hear the latest buzz. The information gained at meetups can be extremely useful because it is localized to your area and job market.

If you live in a large or medium-sized city it will not be difficult to find groups that share your interests. You can check out Meetup.com and search Facebook Groups to see what's available in your area. If you live a distance from the city, it will be harder to justify making frequent trips, but once or twice per month should still be doable. If your situation does not allow for this, there are still live-streamed meetups and even conferences that you can attend virtually. It is more challenging to connect with people, but there is usually a chat or, at least, Twitter hashtags you can use to participate in the conversation.

If you attend one of these events, make sure you get there early and/or stay afterwards to chat with other people. The talks are usually interesting, but the real value comes from in-person meetings and building relationships.

Conclusion

This combination of resources should help keep you up-to-date with your skills and show companies that you know what you are doing. Current knowledge will really come in handy as you network and start getting interviews. While keeping up on what's current has to fit into your schedule, make sure you allocate a set amount of time to spend researching new things since you should be spending most of your time studying and learning.

If you discover other resources for keeping updated with software and tech, please Tweet at me about it, @faraday-academy.

Action Steps:

1. Download a podcast app and subscribe to a few podcasts.
2. Sign up for mailing lists on web development or other topics you are interested in.
3. Decide on a place to keep lists of articles that you want to read later.
4. Search meetup.com and social media sites for local programming groups.

NETWORKING & PUTTING YOURSELF OUT THERE

Section 3

12

BLOGGING

"Blogging is a great way to show your talents and interests to prospective employers while adding an edge to your resume. If you blog consistently, it shows your dedication, passions, and creativity - all of which are key attributes employers look for in job candidates."

— LAUREN CONRAD, POPULAR BLOGGER, AUTHOR

One of the best ways to get your name out there is by keeping a blog. Think of your blog as somewhere to keep all of the details of your foray into programming - your struggles, triumphs, and everything in between. This chapter will cover the "why" and give you all the details you need to start blogging right away.

Why You Should be Blogging

While there are many benefits to blogging, these are the main ones that will align with your goals of learning to code and getting hired:

- Keeping a regular blog can help you track your progress. Imagine working at your dream job several years from now and looking back at the blogs that you are writing now. You are going to be able to look back on your transformation into an awesome engineer detailed step by step. It will also help when you feel down or frustrated; you can look back at all of your progress to remind yourself that you are capable of achieving your goals.
- Blogs are a great way to impress future employers by making you stand out and showing that you are serious about your work. Employers will be able to see what you are learning as well as how you are learning it. As more people see your blog, you may also get job offers or interview requests just from employers reading your posts. Another important thing to remember is that employers will look you up online and blogging is a great way to show them the part of you that you want them to see: that you are dedicated, focused, articulate, and able to explain concepts well.
- You can get feedback on what you are working on, whether that's topics you are studying, projects you are building, or concepts you are stuck on. This is a good opportunity to ask for feedback from your audience at the end of your post. Many people have left me comments or sent me emails that were helpful in making me a better programmer.
- It is a great way to retain the concepts that you are learning. Quincy Larson of freeCodeCamp.org said, "One of the best ways to

reinforce your own learning is to turn around and teach it to someone else, and a technical blog post is an excellent way to do that."

- If you want to freelance or get contracting work, blogs are a great way to do that too. People can get to know you - and to some degree trust you - through your blog. You can use your platform to brand yourself as a thought leader which will lead to speaking engagements, podcast interviews, and other opportunities.
- Finally, blogs are a great way to feel like part of the community and give back. When I was starting out, nothing made me feel better than comments on my articles and blog posts saying that I had helped someone. So many people put themselves out there with awesome content that helped me while I was learning, and it was nice to be able to help others who would follow in my footsteps.

Negative Ideas about Blogging

Some people have negative perspectives about blogging and writing that prevent them from getting started. Here are a few of them:

"No one wants to listen to what I have to say."

"Everything has been said before, how can I contribute something new?"

"I'm not the best writer."

Do not listen to your inner critic! Everyone has lots of valuable insights to share, no matter their experience level, and it does not matter if the topic has been written about once or a hundred times before, you can still lend your own unique voice to the discussion. You do not have to be a good writer to blog but do make sure to use spelling and grammar checks. Like with coding, developing your writing skills also takes repetition and practice.

What Platform Should You Use?

There are three options I recommend for getting started: (1) buy a domain name (e.g. yourname.com), sign up for a hosting service, and install an open source copy of something like Wordpress; or (2) sign up for, and use Hashnode which is a developer specific, managed blogging platform.

It is important to note that there are pros and cons to both options. Here's a breakdown:

	Self-hosted	Hashnode
Cost	~$12 yearly for domain name, $3-5 per month for hosting	Free to start; pay a small amount if you want upgraded features
Customization	Infinite	Limited
Ownership	You	Site is owned by company; content is owned by you
Advertisements	None	Yes
Doman	yourname.com	yourname.hashnode.com or yourname.com

As you can see, hosting it yourself is the more versatile solution. You can customize your own website as much as you want. No one can police what kind of content you post and you always have the option to include ads and affiliate links if you want at any time without worrying about the rules of the platform you are on (they can always change the rules at any time). If you want to host the blog yourself, I recommend using Wordpress or Ghost, they are both easy to setup and use and have robust ecosystems. Personally, I used to use Wordpress on the Bluehost hosting platform for my blog, but switched to hosting Ghost on Digital Ocean over a year ago because I love the interface and speed.

Either option will allow you to have your own name in your domain - like mine, gwenfaraday.com - which makes you look more serious and professional. I highly recommend purchasing one if you have not already.

Hashnode has a beautiful, fully-managed platform specifically made for developer blogs. When you first join, they walk you through a few setup options, prompt you to enter some general information and upload a profile picture, and you are all set to go. Quincy Larsen, the creator of freeCodeCamp recommends the platform, saying, "You can start a blog in just a few seconds using @hashnode and then you can move that to your own domain if you get one later." I completely agree with that statement, it is so easy and quick to get started.

Choose the option that works best for you, as long as you set up your blog as soon as possible. If you want to use a free platform now, you can always move your blog to your own hosting account later.

TIP: Blog Analytics

Wordpress has lots of plugins to easily see how many people are visiting your site and what they are doing while browsing your articles. This can give you very good insight into what is working and what isn't. However, do not get down if your analytics numbers are low; it is completely normal to have almost no visitors for months while you are starting out. I personally used Slimstat Analytics when I had a Wordpress blog, but there are plenty of other options.

Hashnode can actually give you a leg up when you are

starting out because they will try to promote your posts to their audience with similar interests. For example, if you write a Python article, and add the hashtag #python to it, then people like me who follow that hashtag may see your post in our feeds. Hashnode also has primitive analytics and feedback mechanisms so you can see how well your posts are doing.

When you start guest posting your articles (more about this later on in the chapter), some platforms will let you see the analytics for how many of their readers are clicking on your article and how much time they are spending reading it. Check with the platform to see if they can provide you with these details.

Getting Started

What to Write About

Write about yourself and your journey! It doesn't have to be anything mind-blowing or overdone when you are first starting out. Writing more complicated articles or tutorials can come later.

Your first post should be about where you are currently at in your learning, what you are planning to do, and any other relevant details. You want to paint a picture of who you are and where you are coming from for the reader. If you sit down without any distractions, you can easily finish writing this in under fifteen minutes. If you are using Word-press, navigate to "posts" > "add new" on the left menu. You will see a main text area where you can enter the title and body for your blog post. On the right-hand side, you will see a bunch of options that expand to let you enter tags, categories, and other information. You do not have to enter anything there yet, but I recommend adding a featured image if you can.

For subsequent posts, if you can't come up with anything to write about, try answering at least one of the following questions and writing a short post about it.

- What have you been working on?
- What do you want to do with your coding skills?
- What struggles have you encountered?
- Do you have a date or specific goal in mind for getting hired?
- Is there a success story you would like to share?

TIP: Talk about Struggles Without Being Negative

To struggle is human, and it makes you relatable. This journey is full of challenges and it is okay to talk about them openly, but don't be overtly negative in your posts or use your blog as a place to express (or rant) about frustrations you've experienced. Saying things like, "this stinks", "I hate doing this", and "I'll never be any good" isn't a good look for you. That will turn people away from your blog and be harmful when potential employers are reading it. Instead, you can say something like, "sometimes I start thinking that I will not be good at this, but then I remind myself how far I've come and I keep pushing forward" or "I'm really stuck on ABC and I'm feeling pretty frustrated; I'm going to sleep on it and try XYZ tomorrow."

When to Publish

You should aim to publish your blog posts at least one or two times per week. Some people write a new post every day. If that works for you, great. If not, just make a goal to write as often as you can. You do not have to outdo anyone else. It is better to be consistent than burn out.

There is no perfect day or time to publish your blog. However, I recommend that you do not publish more than one at a time. If you write multiple posts at once or close together, you may want to use a scheduling feature (Wordpress and other platforms have this built in) to publish them on certain dates in the future. This also helps if you have a publishing schedule, like every Monday and Thursday; you can write the posts in advance so you never miss your goal.

Taking it to the next level

Writing Articles

Short and personally honest blog posts are great for starting out, but where can you take it from there? A great way to reinforce what you are learning is by writing in-depth articles and tutorials. If you just figured something out, why not write about it so you can understand it more deeply and benefit others at the same time? You do not need to be an expert to write tutorials, either. There are people who can learn from your experiences regardless of your skill level. Blogging is also a great way to connect with beginners who may relate to your struggles more than someone who has been coding for many years.

Writing tutorials and articles that explain concepts also helps brand you as a thought leader. People who write are not necessarily better than those who do not, but they are perceived by others to be more knowledgeable.

The format for this content should include a header, sub-headers, and images, and do your best to be concise. Your audience will be far less likely to read it if there's nothing but blocks of text for them to scroll through.

Here is how I normally approach writing an article:

1. Write a few sentences about the idea and goal of the article. Who is the article intended for and what are they supposed to get out of it?
2. Try to create a catchy title. It should not be clickbait but it should make people want to read the rest of the article. 'How to...', '3 Ways to do XYZ' (lists), and 'Complete Guide to ABC' are all good options. An exercise that can help is to look through popular technology blogs like freeCodeCamp news and Hackernoon to see what titles are popular or stand out.
3. Create subheadings for each section of your article as an outline.
4. Write the introduction. This can just be a paragraph or two about what you will cover in the article and for whom the article was written.
5. Skip to the end and write the conclusion. This section should simply be labeled "Wrap-up" or "Conclusion": no need to have anything fancier than that. People may skim through your article before they read the whole thing and it is good to give them a recap at the end. Since I started writing the conclusion before the body, I've been able to more clearly focus on the end goal throughout the writing process.

6. Write the body under each sub-header.
7. Ask a question at the end of your post. This will get more people to comment and interact with your article.
8. Read through the whole article at least once to catch any simple spelling or grammar errors.
9. Most importantly, send it to a friend or family member to proofread before you publish it. There is a stark difference in the number of spelling and grammar errors I've found in the articles written before versus after I asked someone to double-check my writing. I always use a proofreader for my guest posts now.
10. Publish and share! *More about ways to share your content later in the book.*

For more information about writing good blog posts, see the content for this book at gwenfaraday.com/learn-to-code-book.

Guest Posting

Once every month or two, you should try to guest post your longer tutorials on a publication like freeCodeCamp, Hackernoon, Dev.to, or Software Engineering Daily that have large communities of people interested in anything programming-related. This is an excellent way to get your name out there and build a following without a lot of extra effort?

If you already have a track record of writing on your blog, you can use your previous content as a portfolio in case they ask for links to recent work. Platforms are always eager to post more well-written articles. You should be linking back to your own website and blog from the article to grow your following. Sometimes the platform will have analytics where you can see how many people are reading the article and clicking on the link.

These articles can be on any topic. Here are some ideas to get you started:

1.Write about a problem you recently had and how you solved it.

2.Write about how and why you are learning to code – what techniques you are using, etc.

3.Write an explanation of some part of a programming language or a library you have used.

Conclusion

Blogging can be a valuable tool for people breaking into the tech industry. Push away the negative thoughts and start writing without delay. People will appreciate your honesty and openness. Start as soon as possible and stick with it!

Action Steps:

- Decide where you will house your blog and get it set up.
- Write your first post.
- Schedule the days/times that you will write and post your blogs every week.
- Set reminders and calendar events to keep you on track with your writing.
- Send me a link to your blog by tweeting @faradayacademy. I cannot wait to read it!

13

SOCIAL MEDIA

> "[T]oday's programmers, developers, and code enthusiasts have fully embraced social media. Social media is an incredible vessel for collaboration, sharing, and information discovery, and there are now many great tools that aid in web and software development."
>
> — Ben Parr, mashable.com

In today's world, there are many different types of social media that appeal to various audiences. As a programmer, you will find that some are more equal than others when it comes to networking or being used as learning tools. This chapter will cover the how, what, when, where, and why of using social media to further your goals.

Micro-blogging

Examples: Twitter, Minds.com

The basic idea of these platforms is to follow people and organizations that are interesting to you. While you write

280-character (micro-blogs impose a character limit) posts about whatever is on your mind. The platform then becomes a dynamic RSS feed where you are shown content that is relevant to you based on what you talk about and the people you follow, including news, opinions, discussions, etc. Right now, Twitter is by far the largest micro-blogging platform so it's a good idea to have an account there to connect with people in the industry. As the saying goes, "Twitter is for the people you want to meet."

Connecting with People

In order to network effectively, you will have to ask people to connect with you. As you start meeting people at events, you should exchange Twitter handles (your Twitter name that begins with an '@') with them. If you give a talk at a meetup, ask people to follow you on Twitter. If you have business cards or a personal website make sure you include your Twitter handle with your contact information. It will take some time, but you will start to see yourself building professional connections if you keep working at it.

This isn't only important for seeing current industry news; Twitter can help you find jobs and other opportunities. When a company is looking for talent, many people post about it on Twitter. There are also programs, classes, conferences, and other opportunities that people will Tweet about and that will come up in your feed. I've personally received several freelancing jobs from people who found me on Twitter.

Content

Here are some things you should be posting on Twitter:

- Blog posts you write
- Projects you are working on
- Things you are learning
- Articles and videos you find useful

Making your content discoverable largely depends on smart usage of hashtags on Twitter. Many people and organizations follow, or scroll through feeds of, these hashtags, so you have a much higher chance of people seeing what you posted by using them. Make sure to use appropriate hashtags on most, if not all, of your Tweets. Some examples are adding things like #JavaScript, #webdev, and #nodejs to the end. It's helpful to know that once you start typing a hashtag, Twitter will automatically make recommendations of how to complete it, allowing you to see a filtered list of popular hashtags (make sure you spell it correctly).

When to Post

Since the Twitter feed can really suck you in and turn five minutes into an hour of scrolling, it's good to limit yourself and only log in at scheduled times of the day or while you have just a few minutes to spare. For better time management, you can also schedule your Tweets. I personally use a free service called Buffer for this, but there are many other sites that do the same thing. It works by connecting to your Twitter account, then you type your Tweets into the Buffer interface to be posted on Twitter at a specific time in the future. This also helps if you have several things you want to Tweet about, you can just write them all down and schedule them to go out at different times in the future.

Community

Right now, Twitter has a great developer community: you can see current news in almost real time and Tweet about all the things you are working on for people to see. If you do not have an account, you should sign up right away. The goal is to build your online brand and tell people that you are serious about programming by Tweeting, blogging, etc. If you already have an account, try to make it development-focused as much as you can. It's okay to Tweet an occasional cat or family picture, but you should try to leave out the politically charged or possibly offensive stuff. You never know who is going to look you up online when you start applying for jobs.

Try to Tweet at least every few days about what you are working on and quickly scroll through what influencers are Tweeting about to stay current. Do not be negative or demeaning, orshoot people down. Keep things short, sweet, and positive.

TIP: Taboo Topics

People can misunderstand what you are saying or easily take things out of context on Twitter (the platform is known for this). A few hundred characters or even a series of Tweets is not always the best medium to convey certain opinions or deep thoughts. If you think something you are about to Tweet might be out of place, ask someone for a second opinion before you post it. If you do end up accidentally saying something that people find offensive, sometimes it's best to just delete or rephrase your Tweet to eliminate future confusion.

Q&A Sites, Forums

Examples: Quora, Stack Overflow, Reddit, freeCodeCamp Forum

Stack Overflow is incredibly useful for finding answers to your programming questions, but it can sometimes be brutal if you are asking a question as a beginner. I recommend participating in the freeCodeCamp forum when you need to ask a coding-related question and only using Stack Overflow to search for answers. Both platforms allow you to earn badges and reputation points and progress through levels of trust in the community which can lead to more connections and opportunities in the future. People have received job offers from their outstanding answers on Stack Overflow, but as a beginner, this is highly unlikely. You are better off spending your time studying and building portfolio projects rather than trying to write detailed answers.

Quora is another popular Q&A site in the programmer community. There are lots of great answers and information on the site and they also allow you to build a reputation and get labeled as an "expert" on any topic once you answer enough questions, but keep in mind this status does not mean much when it comes to finding a job or growing your career. If you see a question and can contribute some quality information, do that. Then log off and get back to your studies.

Reddit is a great tool to use for discovering new technologies and ideas that might interest you, learning concepts, or showing off something that you built. You will have to engage in discussions, not just promote yourself. The site is divided up by topics into "subreddits" and there are many of these that relate to programming. Some subreddits to check out: learnprogramming, programming, dailycoding, and freecodecamp.

Chatrooms

Examples: Discord, Gitter

Most large open source projects will have a related chatroom either on Discord or Gitter. Both of these apps are free to use and popular in the open source community. For example, the React.js and Vue.js projects both have Discord chats and freeCodeCamp has a popular community on Gitter. These chatrooms are great for having discussions and are even divided up into rooms that make it easy to post resources, make announcements, and post other content that you do not want to get lost in the main chat feeds.

If you are learning a specific framework like React, that will be a major part of your resume and why someone will hire you, and joining a React-related community chatroom can help you stay up-to-date with announcements, events, updates, problems, etc. Interviewers are always impressed when you know what's current in the technologies you work with.

Other Social Media

Examples: Facebook, YouTube

Facebook is a great place to find local coding groups and events. It's also a place that tempts you to waste many hours scrolling through your home feed. To mitigate this problem, I do not have the Facebook app on my mobile device and I use a browser extension to block access to the site from my computer unless I specifically remove the block. When I need to use Facebook, I unblock it temporarily, check the groups and events I want to check, then re-block it. This helps me stay focused on what I really need to get done instead of mindlessly scrolling.

Speaking of mindlessly consuming content, many people have a similar problem with YouTube. It is easy to have the intention of watching just one tutorial, then realize twenty minutes later that you are already a dozen videos deep in the rabbit hole. If you are struggling with this, I suggest using an internet search engine like Google.com or Duckduckgo.com to look for the videos you want and playing them through the search engine rather than going straight to YouTube. This will help you avoid navigating through screens of distracting suggested content in order to get to the video you really want to see.

None of this is meant to dissuade you from using YouTube. There are many, many great programming channels and tutorials hosted there. Also, video content is a great medium for explaining concepts in lieu of having an in-person professional mentor. There is a large community of programmers that create free tutorials for learners exactly like you. Some good YouTube channels to check out: The Coding Train, freeCodeCamp, Traversy Media, learncode.academy, and, my own channel, Faraday Academy (formerly Coding with Gwen).

TIP: Avoid Wasting Time on Social Media

> "The tycoons of social media have to stop pretending that they're friendly nerd gods building a better world and admit they're just tobacco farmers in T-shirts selling an

addictive product to children. Because, let's face it, checking your "likes" is the new smoking."

— Cal Newport, Digital Minimalism

I already mentioned some tips about focusing, but I want to reiterate here that social media time is not learning time. It's infinitely more valuable to focus and build a project than to interact on social media for hours. If you feel like you might have a problem with wasting time on certain sites, I suggest you keep track of how much time you spend on each site per day and review it cumulatively over the course of a week. An app like Rescue Time can help you with this. (Disclaimer: you might be shocked by the results!) I also highly recommend you read the book, *Digital Minimalism* by Cal Newport where he gives advice on how to overcome digital addictions.

~

Conclusion

Do not underestimate the value of social media on your career but do not waste time on it either. Use the tips I've outlined in this chapter to help you use these platforms effectively.

Action Steps:

1. Sign up for Twitter and start connecting with people.
2. Update your Twitter description to include your learning/career goals.

3. Build a profile on LinkedIn or give your current one a makeover.
4. Ask at least one person to review your social media profiles and LinkedIn to make sure it's professional and paints you in the right light.
5. Use Facebook to search for coding groups and events in your area.

14

LINKEDIN

"It's estimated that one in three professionals on the planet are on LinkedIn. With that kind of reach, you can't afford not to take your LinkedIn profile seriously."

— Vanessa Van Edwards

Linkedin is the most popular professional networking site that provides a great way to get exposure and set yourself up for job opportunities. Thousands of tech companies are looking for potential candidates on the site every day and you want to capture their attention. Here is some advice for filling out your profile and marketing yourself on LinkedIn.

Profile

Your **photo** is the first thing people will see, make sure it is a high-quality, professional or casual photo of yourself. Your face should be clearly visible in the front and center of the image. It is important to smile (or at least look friendly). You want to show that you are serious about your career, and your image speaks volumes to a company about how you present yourself.

The **profile headline** is the next thing people see. It should include your job title or the title of the job you are seeking. If you are trying to get hired as a software engineer, it is okay to put that in your title, even if you do not have a job yet. Imtiaz Ahmad, an Udemy programming instructor, says, "If you are coding every day and expanding your skillsets, you are a software engineer." He advises that the job title is about your profession, not necessarily the job you currently have.

The **summary** section is an overview of your skills and experience. This section should really pique the interest of hiring managers, and is one of the first things people see, so use this space wisely. Include keywords listed like "I am a software developer specializing in JavaScript and web applications." If you are passionate about something related to technology like accessibility or mental health, you can list it here as well. Read it over to ensure you are speaking with your own voice, and avoid nebulous terms like "high performer", etc. Instead, talk about what problems you can help solve for a potential employer.

The **skills and endorsements** section, while not the most important, gives you some credibility and social proof. It is important to list all of the technologies you know here and make sure key items like frameworks and languages are featured at the top. As you build your network, you will notice people start to endorse you for the skills that you list. You should ask people to endorse you when you work with someone on a project or pair program. If you are wondering about what level you need to be at before you list a skill here, a good rule of thumb is to list the technologies that you have worked with in a project once you know the basics fairly well. No need to be expert level.

Your **work experience** should be results-driven and clearly list what technologies you worked on. What have you achieved and what was the impact for the company? Speak with action verbs and talk about achievements. If you build websites or apps for local companies or individuals as you learn, you can put freelance software developer consultant. This will give you some relevant work experience if you do not have anything else to list. If you had to do anything technical at a prior or current job like updating your company's Wordpress blog, highlight that in your work experience. The goal here is not to embellish your skills or be dishonest, but to reframe your current skillset so it fits the tech industry, and see what transferrable skills you already have that can be highlighted in this section that are more technical.

Ask people to give you a public **recommendation** on your LinkedIn profile. Social proof is important and it can mean a lot coming from someone you have worked with, especially from a supervisor. Even though you may feel intimidated or foolish asking for one, many people will be more than happy to write one for you if you ask.

Add your **certificates** to your LinkedIn profile. As you progress through the stages of your learning plan, you will earn certificates from places like freeCodeCamp and Coursera on topics like "front-end", "back-end", and "data visualization". Post these to your profile as soon as you earn them and then announce your achievements to your connections. Never undersell yourself— you are a professional and who is using LinkedIn to let people know what you are capable of.

The **education** section is not only for traditional college experience, but also for students of online curriculums and coding bootcamps. If you are taking classes or going through the curriculum on a site like freeCodeCamp, mark yourself as a student. It will prompt you to add start and end dates, so if you do not know exactly when you will finish, enter in an estimate (you can update it anytime).

Connections

Grow your connections every week. When you exchange information at meetups and events, tell people you will connect with them on LinkedIn. The great thing about gaining connections is that the more you have, the more people will also find you and want to connect, creating a snowball effect. Other ways to grow your pool is by getting involved in relevant groups on LinkedIn. Make sure you join the popular ones related to the field you are trying to get into, e.g. "Web Development". People will be able to find you through your connection to these themed groups.

There are many more profile optimizations for LinkedIn. Ask someone at a meetup to review your LinkedIn profile to get more ideas on how it can be improved.

TIP: Keep your LinkedIn and Resume Consistent

Recruiters and Hiring Managers will compare your resume to what is on LinkedIn, and if they do not match, it can make you seem dishonest, regardless of your intent. Double check to make sure you are using the same job titles, experience, etc.

Conclusion

Do not underestimate the value of social media on your career, but do not waste time on it either. Use the tips I've outlined in this chapter to help you use these platforms effectively.

Action Steps:

1. Build a profile on LinkedIn or give your current one a makeover.
2. Double check that the information on your resume matches your LinkedIn profile.

15

IN-PERSON MEETINGS

"You can't sit back at an event and expect to build connections out of the blue. In order to build connections, you need to get out of your shell and strike up conversations with as many people as possible. Though this is easier said than done, remember that networking is all about hustling and the hardest things in life are the most rewarding."

— Thomas Griffin, from Forbes

Real, human interaction is often undervalued in the tech industry, even though it can have a profound effect on your career. I would not be where I am today without the help of many people I have met over the years at meetups, conferences, and other events. You need to connect with as many people as possible to thrive in this industry. *Note: Because of the 2020 pandemic, many of these events are now being held online. While sometimes it can be hard to have genuine interactions at online events, it still can be done. Try out different groups and events until you find the ones that work the best for you.*

Being shy is not an acceptable excuse to forego networking; I am extremely introverted but I made the effort to get out of my comfort zone and connect with other people at these events. Yes, I had some awkward interactions. Yes, I did not always say the right things. Sometimes I felt anxious after an event. In the end, all of that was peanuts compared to the payoff. Once I realized that other people were just as nervous as me, I was able to get over the fear of introducing myself to new people.

Which Meetups to Attend

There are tens of thousands of tech meetups all over the world, and there will likely be a variety to choose from depending on where you are located. Where I live, there are language-specific meetups for JavaScript, Python, Rust, Go, C#, etc., in addition to more general meetups for things like blockchain, functional programming, or artificial intelligence. There are also meetups that are focused on specific technologies or frameworks like Vue.js, React.js, Django, or Node.js. Finally, there are meetup groups that target specific skill levels and types of people: for example, the local freeCodeCamp chapter targets beginners and Code Black tries to encourage more people of color to learn tech skills.

Which of these should you attend? Start with the ones that most closely relate to what you are learning as well as any groups you identify with and set a goal to attend a few meetings per month. Do not be afraid to attend events that are beyond your skill level, as exposure to more advanced concepts can be very helpful for learning. Do not be afraid to ask questions when you do not understand something. At most meetups, the audience stays pretty quiet and many speakers are happy to receive questions about the topic they are presenting. Asking questions shows you are interested and helps you stand out among the attendees.

Some meetups are less formal and more general. Code and coffees, for example, are usually hosted at a cafe where a group of technologists (mostly programmers) get together to chat about technology-related topics and sometimes work on a light coding project together. You can generally expect to show up at the location, order a beverage, sit down, introduce yourself, tell them about your goals, and get to know everyone. These are great events for connecting and forming relationships with people in your area: I highly recommend checking out as many code-and-coffee-style meetups as possible. Most of them are early in the morning so it might only be possible if you are available (and awake!) and close to an urban area that hosts one of these groups.

How to Find Meetups

There are numerous places to find groups online: meetup.com, Facebook events, even Twitter. It's also good to check out community centers like your local library and any coding bootcamps in your area, as they usually keep lists of relevant events, meetups, and tech groups. Keep a running list of the meetups you are interested in and review them weekly or monthly to see what upcoming events you might be able to attend.

When you meet people at these events, ask them about their favorite local meetups. You may find great communities where you least expect. Just because you are not studying a certain language or framework does not mean those groups will not be helpful to you. Go to the event, even if you do not know the topic, or aren't at the experience level, you can still learn something and connect with other industry professionals. Once you try out several meetup groups, you will have a feel for the communities that best fit your interests and goals.

Networking at Meetups

> "Every man I meet is my superior in some way. In that, I learn of him."
>
> — DALE CARNEGIE, *HOW TO WIN FRIENDS AND INFLUENCE PEOPLE*

When you arrive at a meetup, introduce yourself to anyone in the room and ask them about the technologies they use or something else related to programming. It doesn't matter what you ask them about, just that you start the conversation. People always like to talk about themselves so asking them about what they are doing is a great way to make a positive connection.

Do not forget to ask people for their business cards or contact information and stay in touch; connect with them on Twitter, LinkedIn, and Github if you can. If you have trouble meeting people, make sure to set a goal to introduce yourself to at least two or three new people during the event. If you attend one meetup per week, you will make at least 8-10 new connections per month.

Connecting with people in your local scene is a great way to understand the nuances where you live. For example, if you live in an area where a major company promoted a certain language or technology for a long time, there will probably be a shortage of people who can, or want to, work in those older systems.

When you meet locals who are knowledgeable, well-connected, or interesting, invite them out to coffee or lunch to continue the conversation. You will not only learn a lot, but you will also be more memorable to that person. Speaking of 'connecting with connectors,' the meetup organizers should know who you are. They are usually some of the most well-connected people in the community. By forming relationships, you can also find collaboration partners and mentors who volunteer their time to help people learn. Try to cultivate these relationships with mentors who can advise you on areas and skills you want to develop.

~

TIP: What it is Like as a Minority in Tech

I have been the only female programmer on several teams and one of the minority female tech speakers at many conferences, and I can say that most developers and other professionals I've connected with have done a great deal to help me. Some of the more experienced men I have worked with have donated their time and energy to provide me with feedback and encouragement, for which I am extremely grateful. Sometimes people make out-of-line comments, and you will probably encounter this whether you are a minority in tech or not, but I believe that most instigators are not trying to be hurtful. The best thing to do when you are faced with a situation that makes you uncomfortable is to step back and try to understand where the person is coming from. Fortunately, most meetups, conferences, and organizations will have code of conduct documents and a means of reporting any behavior that can be constituted as harassment.

Most mid-to-large-size companies actively seek out diverse candidates, which can be great if you fit into a minority category. Many minority engineers are recruited heavily first from computer science programs at colleges, which is great for those students. Unfortunately, it also hurts minorities overall since a disproportionate number of them come into the industry from non-traditional backgrounds because they did not go to college, or went for something non-technical and are career changers. The industry is changing, but slowly, and we need to keep encouraging companies to rethink their hiring practices and look for diverse candidates with diverse backgrounds.

Everyone is going through their own journey and feels out of place sometimes. You will meet people, make great connections, and, in turn, help others. If you do not see your particular community represented, start your own group or meetup as I explain below. The best way to make tech more diverse is to start working in it and then encourage your connections to do the same.

Organizing a Meetup

What do you do if there are not many meetups in your area, or the community you are looking for doesn't exist? Start your own. The organizers who run meetups are not any better than you. Maybe they have been in the industry longer, but they do not have your unique personality or appeal to the same communities. Sign up for a free account on Meetup.com or create a Facebook group or do both.

Then start promoting your meetup at every event you go to, hang up flyers about it at your local library or coding bootcamp, and post about it on your local subreddit or community Facebook group.

If you want to start a meetup targeted at a specific demographic or group, then you can apply to become a chapter of a larger non-profit like Women Who Code or freeCodeCamp. They will have branding and some of the details already figured out so it will be easier for you to get started. Many of these groups already have international communities, which will boost your network.

If you live in an area where there are lots of meetups already, consider reaching out to one of your favorites and asking if you can help out. There are lots of ways to help, from finding people who will speaking about a certain topic to being the event host. If there is an online community for the group, you can also help moderate the forum, group page, or chatroom.

Whether you start your own group or volunteer to help one that already exists, it is a great way to start putting yourself out there as a thought leader in the community. It will also help with networking and look great on your resume. Once you get the hang of it, it only takes a few hours per month to organize most meetups.

Conclusion

Even in technology, human interaction is vital for your career. As Jeff Atwood famously said about the importance of humans in software, "No matter what they tell you, it is a people problem."

Action Steps:

1. Make a list of the meetups you want to try.
2. Every month/week review the upcoming meetups and see which ones you will be able to attend. You should shoot for one per week if you live near a city, or at least two per month if they are a farther drive.
3. Set a goal for the number of people you would like to connect with per event.
4. Consider starting your own meetup or helping out with one that already exists.

16

SPEAKING

You do not have to be "TED talk material" or even an experienced programmer to give technical talks. Your presentations do not have to be lengthy or formal either, you can give a quick five minute talk (called a lightning talk) or one that lasts an hour. Public speaking is one of the best ways for your community to get to know you.

Start speaking at events as soon as you can. This is great for resumes and shows people that you can articulate your ideas, regardless of the topic. My first talk was teaching people why and how to create blogs about their path to learning software development. We spent some time going over the benefits of having their own blog and then I had everyone sign up on Wordpress.com to create one right on the spot. We made a master list of the web addresses for everyone's blogs so we could check up on each other and send encouragement. The talk turned out well even though I didn't have a single line of code in the presentation.

Do not let your fear of public speaking get in the way. The keys to getting over that fear are preparation and practice. This chapter goes over how to get started with speaking at local events and growing into presenting at larger technical conferences.

How to Get Started

I recommend starting by finding a local meetup like Python or JavaScript or freeCodeCamp and asking them if they will let you present on something for a set amount of time. You could start by simply showing off a project you are working on for five to ten minutes and talking about your struggles and victories and what you learned. People want to hear your ideas. If you are open about your struggles, they will also be able to relate to you.

After the talk, always ask for feedback and give people a way to reach you via email and social media. Tell the room about your plans and what stage you are at in learning to code. You will get a lot of encouragement and support from doing this.

You will become more comfortable each time you speak. After the first couple of times, try creating a full-length technical talk, maybe something like "Intro to React.js" or "An In-depth look at Regex." Shoot for 30-45 minutes of content, and make sure to leave time at the end for questions. It's much easier to practice and prepare for a talk that is 30 minutes versus one hour or longer. If you finish early, ask the audience if they have any questions or bring up a new feature (related to the topic you presented on) that just came out and ask your attendees to discuss the pros and cons. If you can, always try to make part of the presentation interactive, even if it just means having a Q&A session at the end or asking people for their feedback or thoughts on the presentation.

After you are more comfortable speaking at local meetups, where do you go from there? Apply to speak at regional, national, and then international conferences!

How to Speak at Conferences

Conferences can be stressful even if you are not presenting, but speaking at one can really boost your career, help you network, allow you to travel for (almost) free, and give back to others at the same time.

I've given over a dozen conference talks in the last few years, so the following sections come from my own experience as well as the advice I've received from other experienced public speakers.

Applying to Conferences

Since it can be difficult to get accepted to your first conference, I recommend speaking at local events first. The people who run those groups are always happy to have volunteer speakers and the audience is much more forgiving when you are starting out. This is also a good way to meet conference speakers who can put in a good word for you with conference organizers. If you do not know any conferences speakers yet, announce at the end of your talks that you are looking for connections in the conference speaking world, and you are almost sure to get some leads.

It's also a good idea to try to record at least one of the local talks you give so you can use it on conference applications. Some local meetups have recording equipment already, so you can either find one of those meetings or find someone with their own equipment to borrow if you do not own any yourself. Over the last four years, I have had many of my meetup's members offer to loan me recording equipment and I am sure you can find someone with a simple video camera and a cordless mic or two if you just ask.

Before speaking at my first conference, I made lots of connections by presenting at local meetups and events. This not only helped me to boost my confidence, but also improve my speaking presence - eye contact, vocal projection, etc. These skills are important to develop before beginning to speak at conferences. After a few local talks, someone that I met recommended that I apply for a new, local conference. I applied and got in! Then one talk led to another and I started to get accepted at, or invited to, increasingly more domestic and international conferences.

Here are some conferences I recommend applying to first:

1. Conferences where you have networked to get your foot in the door. If you know someone who can recommend you to the organizers, it is like starting off on the 50-yard-line for a 100-yard sprint.
2. Any local conference—They love to attract local speakers because it is, A: cheaper, and B: better for local advertising and promotion. You can also usually connect with the people who run it beforehand and ask them to give you a chance as a first-time speaker.
3. NDC conferences—These are very well-run conferences that are hosted all over the world. They pay for your airfare, hotel, meals and some events, meals, and free admission to the conference. It is not just about the free stuff

though, they attract top notch speakers and a wonderful community of people. I have personally been to NDC conferences in London, Sydney, and Minnesota. I plan on applying for many more in the future, so maybe I will see you at one soon!

4. Python conferences—The Python community is known for being very open and welcoming to newcomers. Many of the conferences are low cost or free and you can sign up to give a five minute lightning talk if you just want to get your feet wet. The people at all of the Python conferences I've been to are so nice and will try to help you and give you feedback on what you can do better.

Making a Proposal

Once you find a conference you want to apply to, you have to write a proposal for the talk and come up with a title. Most of the time, the requirements will be similar or the same so you can pretty much copy/paste to reuse talk proposals. Here are some general steps to making good proposals:

1. **Research the topic:** Usually, you can see a list of the speakers and talks from previous years on the conference website (unless it's the first year, of course). Take note of about what people spoke about and which topics were underrepresented. Most of the speaker profiles will also link to contact information, so you can reach out to individual speakers and ask them their opinion

on the conference and for advice on applying and getting accepted. If you are coming up with a new talk for the conference, I highly recommend connecting with speakers from previous years before you write your proposal. They will usually have insight into the kinds of talks that are most likely to get accepted at that particular conference. Keep in touch with them so you can ask for a review of your talk proposal as well.

2. **Make a catchy title:** The title is the first—and sometimes only—thing attendees see when they are scrolling through a list of talks online or in the brochure at the event. It has to grab their attention, so conference organizers look for great titles when they are reviewing talks. Pick out some of the titles that pop out at you when you scroll through talks from previous years and keep a list of them for inspiration as you are making your proposals.
3. **Create a proposal:** Make a quick list of things you will cover and in what order. Write down an overview of what the talk will be about and then make notes about what you want the audience to get out of the talk. Experienced speakers have always told me to talk to the audience in the proposal and tell them how they will directly benefit from attending. From reviewing lots of talk descriptions in the past, I have found that starting the description with a question can pique interest. Here is an example: "What if we could build apps that are not just functional, but also fun to use? Done right, gamification can vastly improve user experience as well as

boost…" Some conferences will ask you to do an abstract as well as a description and some will ask only for a description and then truncate it if they need a shorter version. Either way, the method of writing the proposal takes about the same amount of time.

4. **Ask someone to review it:** Several experienced speakers have helped me a lot over the years from reviewing my talk proposals, to giving me advice, to helping me practice. It can never hurt to ask someone for help. The title of my last conference talk, "Game on! Gamifying your apps for fun and profit."—and the idea for making it—came from another speaker I met years ago who has helped me with encouragement and advice for almost every talk I have given.
5. **Save your proposal:** Many conferences manage their proposals with something like Sessionize.com or PaperCall.io so you can log back in and look at them in the future. Some conferences, however, have their own forms that you will not have access to, so it's best to save the title, abstract, description, tags, and any other information you enter in a separate location just in case.

Rejection

Everyone gets rejected. It happens all the time, even to experienced speakers. You never know if it was because you are a new speaker, or because the topic did not fit in with one of the tracks, or they might have had too many people applying to give similar talks. It is not personal, keep applying and you will get in somewhere. A good strategy when you are starting out is also to apply for multiple talks and then make a note that you only want to give one or two of the talks at the conference. That gives the organizers a chance to pick the ones they think will be the most enticing to attendees and you have a much higher chance of at least one of your talks getting accepted.

Planning & Preparation

Practice the talk at local meetups first. If you have already been accepted, then you have to prepare the talk anyways—you might as well use it more than once! Reach out to local coding groups, coding bootcamps, or companies, many companies love to host "lunch and learns", and ask for feedback at the end. This will also push you to finish your talk materials early and give you time to iterate on them before the conference.

When I am accepted for a conference, I like to make a map of what I have to get done and by when. Preparing for a talk is not easy. There is research to do, code to write, and slides to make. If you do not plan and start working in advance, the time for the conference will arrive with you scrambling to get everything done. This makes an already stressful situation even more stressful.

Every talk will be different, but I generally find myself following similar steps to prepare. For example, I usually make a list of relevant articles and books to read right away because that takes the longest. Once I have done some research and have lots of notes, I go through them and write out a detailed outline of what I will cover in the talk. Then, I decide what framework I want to use for my slides, and if I can reuse styles from someone else's template, all the better.

After that, I make some placeholder slides for each section of my talk and then work to fill in the details. *Note: It's a good idea to keep the description of your talk nearby where you can see it while preparing for your talk. This will help to make sure your content doesn't diverge from what you promised the conference and your audience.*

Once I have the talk and slides almost ready, I start practicing it. This helps me find holes and inconsistencies that I might not notice while creating individual slides and sections one at a time. If the talk is longer than 30 minutes, it can be hard to practice the whole thing several times. In that case, I shoot for at least 3–6 complete run-throughs, depending on how well I know the topic. When you are practicing a long talk, it is easy to get distracted in the middle and not start back up from the same place you left off, so it is important to practice not only the beginning, but the middle and ending as well.

In addition to preparing your talk, here are a few items to remember to bring with you to the conference:

1. Prepare cables for your laptop and any dongles just in case the conference doesn't have the right ones for your setup (most will, but you never know).
2. Store a copy of your slides and any code in the cloud or on a thumb drive just in case something happens to your computer. If you are using slides.com, google slides, or something similar, they have the ability to export as html or pdf files.
3. If you are doing any sort of live coding, you should probably have a video or slideshow backup. All sorts of things seem to happen when

you are on stage and it never hurts to be extra prepared. Video backups have saved me a few times.

4. Always have business cards to give out after the talk in case there is someone you want to connect with.

Arriving at the Conference

When the conference rolls around, the best thing is to arrive at least a day early and get situated. This can help relax your nerves and feel more confident. I like to check out the conference venue in advance and make sure I know how to get there. I was late for one of my talks once because I got lost in a new city trying to get to the conference. I felt terrible about it for the rest of the trip. Make sure you prepare early and do not make this mistake.

When you arrive at the conference venue, the first thing you will see is an information desk where you can check in and receive a speaker name tag or badge and whatever official swag they are giving out. If the room you are speaking in isn't marked on your name tag, make sure to ask them so you know where it is and are not scrambling at the last minute.

As a speaker, you will probably have access to a few rooms that other attendees do not. Most conferences have a tech check room where you can plug in your laptop ahead of time. Make sure you ask about this at the info desk if you can't find where it is. There will also be a speaker room for you to work on your talk and relax or chat with other speakers. This is probably the best place to go to meet people when you initially get there. It's a relaxed environment and it's great to start networking with other people in the speaker circuit as soon as you can.

When I started going to conferences, I would hide in my hotel room during meals if I did not know anyone.Now I make myself sit at a table with other people and start a conversation, and in most cases the people I sit down with are usually just as awkward and nervous as myself. I have met lots of cool people by just sitting at a table with them and asking a few simple questions.

On Stage

If you are introverted, it can feel extremely overwhelming knowing you are about to go on stage and start speaking. In the past, I sometimes experienced panic attacks before giving talks. It's just something you have to push through if you want to become a good speaker. Remember, everyone wants you to succeed, especially your audience. I like to go into the bathroom beforehand and take a few deep breaths. Then I arrive at least 10–15 minutes early to get set up in the room where I will give my talk. This will really help to calm your nerves.

I once listened to a talk by Robert C. Martin—author of *Clean Code*—and asked him for speaking advice afterwards. He told me that I have to believe that I am the expert in the room and the audience is stuck there listening to me no matter what, so I might as well have fun with it. It was a simple thing to say, but that advice made an impression on me and my speaking improved after that.

Remember, it doesn't have to be perfect. Everyone has good and bad speaking days. It can be a good idea to lead off the talk by saying that it's your first conference and that you really appreciate XYZ conference for allowing you to come and speak. It's always a good thing to start off by getting your audience to relate to you somehow, and that will probably make you feel more comfortable too.

If I have more than a few minutes left at the end of my talk, I will ask the room for questions and try to answer them in front of everyone. Otherwise, I will wrap up and tell attendees that I would love to answer their questions or talk to them afterwards.

There may be times when you only have a few or even no attendees. I've personally seen this happen to two very experienced speakers. Sometimes, it's a topic that people aren't interested in, or there is another famous speaker scheduled at the same time as you, or it was just a bad time of day (early in the morning after people went out the night before, or at the end of the day when people are worn out). Do not feel bad, if it happens, make sure you wait 10-15 minutes and then either stay in the room to practice your talk anyways or take the opportunity to see someone else's presentation.

Afterwards

You are done! Almost... Be sure to stay around for questions and discussion. If there is another talk after yours in the same room, just say you'll be in the hallway after. It's a great feeling to finish and then have people tell you thanks and give you compliments.

Do not forget to thank the conference organizers for allowing you to attend and give a talk. If you do not want to do it in person, a "thank you" email is great too. Tweet or write about your experience on your blog.

Conclusion

Do not be afraid to speak at meetups and conferences. It's a great way to improve your speaking skills, network with lots of new people, and travel, among other benefits. I hope to meet many of you at conferences in the future. If you are going to give a conference talk, please Tweet about it so I can see: @faradayacademy.

Action Steps:

1. Reach out to a meetup organizer and ask to present about a project you are working on.
2. After the first few presentations, prepare a talk and schedule to give it at a local meetup.
3. Apply to speak at your first conference.
4. Leverage your conference speaking experience to give talks at more conferences and continue speaking!

17

BRANDING YOURSELF

"Even if you don't think you have a brand, you do. It is what people think of you and the work you do... Your brand is the conversation going on about you while you are not in the room. The question is: do you know what your brand is and are you managing it?"

— Andria Corso, workitdaily.com

What is branding? It is the story you are selling about yourself. It is curating the information that exists about you to align with your values and goals. It is all about being crisp, uniform, and crystal clear.

How you come across to people is important as you break into the software industry and look for your first job. Your message should be easy to understand and consistent across every platform where people might find you (including in-person). You are a professional and your branding should convey that to people.

For what do you want to be known? What do you want

people to see when they search for you online? You should carefully consider the answers to these questions as you develop your personal brand as a software engineer.

Creating Your Brand

Figuring out what your brand is should not be a difficult task, do not overcomplicate it. A good way to get started is to write out a list of what you are looking for in a job, what types of coding you are focusing on, and what makes you unique as a software developer and a person. Write down a list of these words or phrases, draw pictures or symbols, etc.

Once you have this list, combine synonyms and then circle the items that most closely align with your goals. Does everything you circled reflect not only who you are, but also who you want to be? Good! Now you are ready to move on.

You will need to create a summary of your brand. Start by writing out a few sentences about yourself using the keywords (or pictures, etc.) you chose on your list. These sentences should answer the questions of who you are (e.g. "A software developer", "entrepreneur", etc.), what you are doing (e.g. 'focusing on React.js and front-end'), and your goal (e.g. 'Looking for job opportunities'). Remember to avoid platitudes or nebulous terms; people can sense if it is not genuine. Once you have these keywords and sentences, ask yourself if the brand distinguishes you and showcases your uniqueness: Does it stand out? Does it highlight your skills and what you are trying to accomplish? Does it sound professional? Does it showcase your personality?

On your blog and other platforms, you will probably be writing about how you are learning to code and all of your struggles, etc. That's fine to present yourself as someone who's new and eager to learn and make mistakes. However, when you have studied for at least a few months, or a minimum of 250 hours, you really have to start branding and pitching yourself as a professional or it will be hard for companies to take you seriously. The key is to be open about your learning process while still showing that you are a professional problem solver. Be very vigilant of the language you are using to refer to yourself.

Important: You should call yourself a software developer or engineer. You should not include the words "junior", "aspiring", "hopeful", or anything of the kind in your personal brand. You have put in the sweat equity to learn and build your portfolio and now you need to brand yourself as the professional that you are. People almost never want to hire someone who isn't confident or who conveys they "might" be able to do something in the future. You need to exude confidence and sell yourself. Remember that you are just as good and as dedicated as anyone else in the industry, just with less experience.

Logo

An important part of branding is consistency. It is important to have a consistent message across your social media, portfolio website, blog, and business cards. A great way to do that is by having a consistent logo. It doesn't have to be fancy; you can just create something simple like your name or initials with a background behind it. Canva is a great online tool that will let you create a decent quality, simple logo for free. Another option is to pay someone to make one that looks a bit nicer for you. Fiverr.com is a freelance marketplace where people from all over the world sell design and other services, and you can have a logo created within a few days for about $10-$25. If you go this route, make sure you have a friend look it over for you to get a second opinion before you accept the final design in case you need to ask for revisions.

Creating or commissioning a logo should not take you more than an hour or two. This is not the most important part of your learning and you should not sweat about it being perfect. A decent logo is a great start; you can always update it later when you have landed a sweet job and are looking for the next step.

Profile Photo

Your photo is usually the first thing people see on any of your online profiles. I suggest using a professional-looking image of your head and shoulders. Smiling also helps people feel more comfortable with you. Fair or not, humans make categorical judgements about others within milliseconds. If you look professional and friendly, that will go a long way.

People will also start to recognize you more easily if you use the same picture across all of your platforms. Humans also naturally put more trust in people they recognize, so that can give you a leg up.

Business Cards

Once you are dedicated to learning to code and pursuing programming as a career, you should really consider getting your own business cards. There are websites like Vistaprint.com and Moo.com that allow you choose between hundreds of templates, plug in your information, and then order hundreds of business cards for a low cost - $20 gets you 500 cards on Vistaprint.

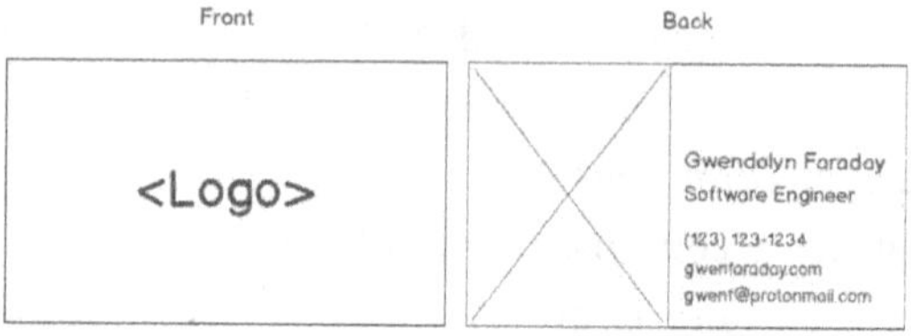

Of course, the main point of a business card is the contact information, so that should be easy to read, front and center. It is also a nice touch to include your profile photo as long as it is recent and professional. This photo usually looks nice next to your contact information on one side of the card, with your logo on the other side. Using a template will help you with getting the layout correctly formatted and making the card look professional. If you do not have a logo, and you have a good eye for design, you can also use some kind of sharp-looking clip art on one side; I have been using a stylized smiley face on the front of my business cards and have gotten a substantial amount of compliments from it. If we ever meet in person, I will be happy to give you one of my cards so you can see.

Online

Check every platform you are on - Twitter, LinkedIn, Github, your portfolio site, etc. - and update your info to include your brand summary. You may have to make it shorter on sites like Twitter where most people describe themselves in 25 words or less. Remember to update your profile photos to match as much as possible and look professional.

You should also include a call to action at the end of your brand summary like, "check out my portfolio at example.com and get in touch with me." Another good touch is to include your logo in your banner or somewhere else on each of your profiles.

You can also generate awareness for your brand through networking and creating content. Your blog posts, tweets, and everything you post online should align with your brand and how you want other people to see you. Make sure your blog posts are proofread and everything you do comes across as crisp and professional. Simple mistakes like typos can make a big difference in how people perceive you, even if your content is great.

Your Pitch

You have to be able to sell yourself when you meet people or converse electronically via LinkedIn, email, etc. In politics, they tell candidates to have a 30-second "elevator pitch" that clearly describes their platform. As a job candidate, you should do the same thing; craft a short pitch that describes who you are and what you want to do. It doesn't have to use eloquent language, but it should be easy to understand and to the point about your goals.

Look through everything you wrote down previously and tweak your sentences so they sound natural when spoken aloud. You may be able to use exactly what you wrote earlier for your brand summary in your pitch, and the primary goal is to sell yourself and be confident.

Practice makes perfect and breeds confidence. Every time you meet someone, have lunch with a recruiter, or give a technical talk, you should be ready with your polished pitch. Ask your mentor, friends, or family to listen to your spiel and give you feedback. You should have it down so you will be able to deliver it even when you are nervous or caught off guard.

Conclusion

Do not be afraid to brand yourself as a professional. Many people do not like the idea of marketing themselves and end up selling their abilities short. You have to start viewing and presenting yourself as a confident professional who can overcome challenges to reach your goals.

Action Steps:

1. Brainstorm and write about who you are and your goals.
2. Come up with a brand summary.
3. Review your social media to make sure it fits with your brand and make changes as necessary.
4. Create a logo.
5. Prepare a professional photo of yourself.
6. Buy business cards.
7. Create a pitch, then practice and refine it.

18

NETWORKING

"There are three ways to ultimate success. The first way is to be kind. The second way is to be kind. The third way is to be kind."

— Fred Rogers (Mr. Rogers)

We have covered networking briefly in previous chapters, but I want to take a deeper dive here since it is such an important part of landing your first job. Referrals are still the number one way to get your foot in the door at a new company. Not only that, but they will also let you know about other companies that are hiring so you can go and apply. The more people you positively interact with, the higher your chances of making the right connection that will lead to employment.

Since networking deals with humans instead of computers, this topic is much more delicate and complex than learning to code on its own. This chapter will cover some of these intricacies and give some tips on dealing with the toughest - and most important - part of software development: people.

Where to Network

You only have so much time in your schedule to do all of your learning, and then there's networking stacked on top of that. To do both effectively, you have to do a little planning to figure out where your energy will be best spent. Some events might be enjoyable, but not very fruitful in helping you meet the right people for finding your first job. You want to start attending events where there will be people who can help you achieve your goals.

Let's spend some time going over each type of event to network at, and the type of people to connect with at each one.

Coding Groups

This is the first type of event you will probably attend to build relationships when you are a beginner. These groups usually meet weekly or monthly and you can find them by looking on Meetup.com, Facebook Groups, etc. They are great places to meet other developers of all levels and start to make friends who can recommend you for jobs later.

When you are seriously looking for jobs and have decided on the type of company you want to work for, make an effort to connect with people at events who work at these companies. Invite them out to coffee with you. You should ask them what they like or dislike about the company, what their responsibilities are, what their schedule is like, and any other information that is important to you in considering employment.

If you have picked out a list of specific companies you would like to work for, try to find their employees on LinkedIn and Twitter. See if they post about specific group meetings or events that they are going to attend. Look at the companies' job postings on LinkedIn or their career pages. If you can see what tech stacks they use (and you will usually be able to find that information just by searching online), then you know which meetups to start checking out in order to connect with their employees.

Tech Events

There are many one-time, annual, or finite series events with technical or entrepreneurial focuses. The themes will vary widely, but some examples are diversity in tech, business-related seminars, and technical workshops. You might find these events hosted by local libraries, community centers, churches, or non-profit groups in your area. Search on sites like Eventbrite, which is a great place for finding one-off events, since they are usually not hosted by monthly user groups that you would find on Meetup.com.

These events offer you the opportunity to meet people who run companies, who are not always programmers. So many people get stuck in a bubble of always being around software engineers, and they likely will not be the best connections as far as employment goes. You have to get out of your comfort zone.

Conferences

Tech conferences generally last between two and five days, although some specialized ones can be only one day. The conference schedule is packed with six to eight talks per day and one or two full days of workshops with back-to-back with short breaks to get from one talk to the next. They almost always have nightly activities too, like dinners, game nights, nerd comedy (yes, it is both popular and funny for tech workers), or parties.

While conferences can have thousands of attendees, you will find that people usually fit into just a few categories. Many medium-to-large companies will pay for their employees to attend to receive training for new skills, make connections, recruit, and get fresh ideas. There are also tech start-ups who attend with the goals of handing out their business cards and getting more people to sign up for their services. Then there are those who go by themselves or with other people from a local meetup group looking for training, networking, and jobs. Finally, there are speakers and workshop hosts who get to go for free in exchange for presenting at the conference.

I highly recommend networking with this last group of people as much as possible. Conference speakers are usually well-connected, and most of the time they have a big influence on recruiting and hiring at their companies. Before you attend the conference you should try to have the talks you want to attend picked out so you know where to go and do not have to waste time in the hallways making those decisions. Take the time to look up the speakers for the talks you are going to attend and see if you can find mutual interests or come up with questions that you want to ask them. After the talk, approach them and start a conversation. If they are local, try to get them to meet you for coffee, but either way, make sure you get their business card and follow up with them online.

One other group of people you want to look for are developer advocates. These people are paid by their companies to promote their technologies. Usually, they have good social skills and are looking for diverse candidates to recruit for their companies.

While you're there, try to stop at every booth set up at the conference. Some of them will be trying to sell something but most of them are there to recruit talent. If you are shy, just practice one intro that you will use with every booth, such as, "Hi, I'm a software developer and I'm curious about your company, could you tell me more about what you do." Keep asking questions and engaging, especially if you are interested in working there. Do not forget to get contact information and exchange business cards.

Meal times are not the time to sit by yourself unless you really feel like you need to take a break. These are the best times to network. If you see a speaker or someone you wanted to talk to but didn't get a chance to yet, go and sit with them. Do not let things be awkwardly silent either. Ask them questions about themselves and they will love talking with you. Practice really listening and engaging and, like Dale Carnegie says, they will think you are a great conversationalist.

A big non-starter for beginners is the price tag of conferences. Most of the time you can ask for a discount, but it will only be 10-20% off, which is still expensive. A good way to get around the price tag is to offer to volunteer. Usually, conferences only require you to work for one day to get a free ticket to attend the whole conference. Being a volunteer means you get to network with all of the people running the conference behind the scenes. Use that to your advantage and ask the organizers if you can speak at the next one. If you are there early or late as a volunteer, you may also get the opportunity to network with speakers during off times while there aren't many other people at the venue.

Awards Ceremonies

These events are less common, but you can find the "who's who" of connected individuals in your community at these types of events, and it's a great place to network if you can attend. Wear something nice, bring your business cards, and be as friendly as possible. The same networking rules apply as other types of events, and take the extra initiative to follow up with the connections you make as they are all probably busy with their careers.

Entrepreneurship Classes & Groups

You will find many business owners and aspiring business owners at these types of events. These are exactly the type of people you want to connect with. If you can form relationships with some of them, they might take a chance on hiring you for your first software development role on a small team where you can ask lots of questions and make lots of mistakes.

If there are entrepreneurship classes being offered at your local library or community center, try signing up for them. Usually, the time commitment and costs are low, and you will learn a lot about your options for starting a company. Also, most importantly, you can make great connections with other motivated people who might hire you when they start their own companies.

Networking & Social Events

Many events are created solely for the purpose of networking with no other presentations or objectives. Some examples of these types of events are tech happy hours, holiday socials, and start-up/small business networking events. Be careful going to these though, if you do not plan and go in with a strategy, then you might just end up talking the whole time and not getting much out of it.

Make it a point to go to the ones that have something to do with tech, startups, or entrepreneurship. Regular social events outside of these genres seem to be mostly for making friends, partying, and matchmaking (from my experience anyways). Before you attend, look up the event and see if you can find a list of people who have RSVP'd. Search for them on LinkedIn and make note of the ones you want to talk with during the event.

Be sure to arrive at these types of events as early as possible. It is much easier to speak with people when you are one of a few versus after people have already formed groups later on and you have to figure out how to insert yourself. If you do not have anyone to talk to at the moment, scan the room and look for people at the edges who might be by themselves. Go and strike up a conversation. After fifteen minutes or so, exchange information and politely excuse yourself and look for the next person to talk to. This strategy will maximize the people you can make an impression on during the few hours that you have at the event.

Hack-a-thons

At hack-a-thons, try to connect with other people as much as possible and introduce yourself to the people who come to watch the presentations at the end as they are sometimes looking to hire. If there are mentors who are available to help you, then make sure you exchange information with them as well and follow up online after the hack-a-thon ends.

Online

There are tons of interest groups on sites like Facebook and LinkedIn where you can meet people. While there are many potential connections to be made, it is also easy to get distracted online so you have to guard your time and make sure you do not get carried away scrolling through feeds.

I recommend starting by finding some groups on Reddit, Facebook, or LinkedIn that align with your career goals and join them. You want to be around the people who are where you want to be as much as possible and it is easier to do this online. Every few days, look through the feeds and like or comment on a couple of posts. If you find an article or resource that you think might interest that group, post it. As you interact with more people, try to find opportunities to ask for recommendations in companies.

How to Network with People

Nobody gets hired in a vacuum. It is not only important to meet people, but to practice social skills and awareness. Here are some tips on how to interact with people at events to maximize your effectiveness as you are trying to get your first job.

Types of People

There's a whole spectrum of people between introverted and extroverted, with most people lying somewhere in the middle. If talking to strangers intimidates you, try starting out with the other shy people sitting in the back or standing at the edges of the room. Once you get used to initiating conversations, it will become easier and you can progress to talking to everyone in the room.

Breaking the Ice

The best thing you can do to sound confident is to not hesitate. Insert yourself by greeting the person or people and asking a question right away if possible.

Just start by saying "hi" and grinning or giving a friendly smile. Then follow up by asking a question like, "What did you think about the presentation?" or, "What industry do you work in?" In some instances, it is not considered good manners to ask a stranger about their employment, but at a tech meetup, it is an acceptable topic of conversation. Refrain from asking questions like, "How are you?" because they usually lead to one-word answers like "good" and then it can stifle the conversation if you are already nervous or awkward.

Keeping it Classy

You might find this obvious, but do not talk negatively about other people or be antagonistic toward someone else's point of view. Try to steer the conversation toward events, activities, technologies, etc. You may get accidentally roped into a conversation where someone unabashedly expresses their views on a certain technology, sometimes to the point that makes others uncomfortable. If that happens, be polite and absorb the information, and try to remain neutral until the topic has passed.

Try to ask lots of questions and show interest in who you are talking to. Being on top of your game in terms of manners and etiquette will score big points for you when people are thinking about giving referrals or companies are considering cultural fit for hiring.

Correctly RSVP "yes" or "no" as appropriate. If something comes up, change your RSVP status as soon as possible. As a meetup organizer myself, I cannot tell you how frustrating it is sometimes that people RSVP "yes" all the time and do not show up.

Maximize your Time

If it is a large event, you want to limit your time talking to each person. As I mentioned before, 15 minutes is a good amount of time to get to know someone and exchange information. You can keep the conversation going online later on, or by scheduling a coffee date in the future. Do not only talk to the same people or people you feel comfortable around. To be successful at networking, you have to branch out and force yourself to meet new people, even if that seems intimidating.

How to Politely End Conversations

Sometimes conversations can get to a point where they are no longer productive, and if a conversation is going on too long, say something like, "I really enjoyed getting to know you. I want to chat with a few more people right now. Can we exchange information and stay in touch?" Say goodbye, shake hands, and walk away, that is all there is to it. Sometimes I think we are afraid that being direct or removing yourself from the conversation can come across as impolite, but if you take control of the situation, there will not be an opportunity for awkwardness. I personally practiced conversation skills like this in front of the mirror to make sure I was on point when the occasion arose.

Other Recommendations

- Some obvious things: Always wear something that is clean and looks nice. You will stand out if you look sharp. You want to look serious but not stuffy and overdressed.
- Remember that your first priority is finding a job. Always ask for the opportunity to interview. If you meet someone at a company you want to work for, ask them to connect you with the hiring manager.
- Do not be shy, promote yourself and what you are doing to your whole network. You need to be confident. If they have introductions at the start of the event, then announce to the whole room that you are looking for a job as a software developer. You may be surprised how many people want to help.
- Remember to be friendly and offer to help. It is not only a gracious act, but it will also benefit you greatly. People are much more likely to help you if you help them, even in a small way.
- Read the book, *How to Win Friends and Influence People* by Dale Carnegie for more tips on human interaction.

Conclusion

Get out there and network as much as your schedule allows: at least once per week if possible. Meet people who are where you want to be and from companies where you want to work.

Action Steps:

1. Plan events on your calendar every week or month.
2. Correctly RSVP and show up early if possible.
3. Remember to bring business cards.
4. Keep control of conversations and meet as many people as possible.
5. Tell everyone that you are (or will soon be) looking for a job.
6. Do not forget to follow up with people you met within 48 hours. Send them a note and connect with them on LinkedIn and other social media platforms.

JOB PREPARATION

Section 4

19

PORTFOLIO

"Years ago, only artists and other creative professionals had portfolios. These days, *every* professional can benefit from having one... The real purpose is to provide tangible proof of your value in the workplace."

— CHRISSY SCIVICQUE, THEMUSE.COM

Having a portfolio where potential employers can see the projects you have been working on is tremendously important. You do not need a college degree or be a coding genius, but you *do* need to show that you have a current, hirable skillset. The best way to do that is with an online personal portfolio showcasing projects you built using relevant technologies. In this chapter, we will dive into the details of how to create one for yourself and what you should include in it.

What is a Developer Portfolio?

A developer portfolio is a webpage that shows a list of the projects you have worked on with links to any live apps you are hosting as well as the code you have written for them. You should also include other types of related experience such as links to talks you have given, open source projects you have contributed to, video tutorials or workshops you have recorded and hosted somewhere like YouTube, and a place with all of your contact information so people know how to reach you. This portfolio is akin to an e-resume that highlights your projects first, and other proof of your experience, it is a living, breathing website to show off your skills that will keep changing as you grow.

Go search for "developer/software engineer portfolio" and look through some examples. Take note of how they are laid out, what information is displayed, and how they are displaying it. While the examples you find may be of varying quality, looking through these will help you get an idea of what you want to include as you build your own portfolio.

Don't worry, your first portfolio does not have to be anything advanced, it just needs to be clean, easy to read, and not cluttered. You can make it look nice and modern just by using enough white space and good fonts (like Open Sans, available for free from Google Fonts). Or you can use your Github profile as I detail below.

On my website, I also have a blog post of well-designed portfolio examples for you to check out. Some of them are more creative than others; the list is just there to give you some ideas. If you want to see examples of my portfolios that I used in the past, check out my YouTube video on the topic: youtube.com/watch?v=qcOfJIcKfMk.

Using Github for a Portfolio

The easiest way to create a good developer profile now is to use your Github account. Github now allows so many ways of customizing your profile page with a README at the top, the ability to pin projects, and a section for showing off your work in the community.

I have always had a separate portfolio in the past, but now, even I do not see an advantage to creating an extra website to house my portfolio. Github gives me everything I need and has saved me a lot of time from building and managing a custom portfolio page. Here is my Github profile if you want to take a look: github.com/gwenf.

Here are the steps I recommend for setting up your Github profile:

1. Create a readme: If you notice, the top of my profile page has a section where I say, "Hi, my name is Gwen..." That is a README.md file that I created specifically to display on my page. You can make one too just by creating a repository on Github with the same name as your username. When you are creating it, just check the "Initialize this Repository with a README file" box. Then edit the README with the markdown text, images, and emojis that you want and save it. And you are down! You should now have a working README at the top of your Github profile page. Here is the repository that my README comes from if you want to take a look: github.com/gwenf/gwenf.
2. The basics: Use your real name and a professional-looking profile image.

3. Pin your best projects in the "Pinned" section right below the README you just created.
4. Fill in your green squares: Keep committing code to Github to make a consistent track record; think small and frequent commits.
5. Do you have any impressive contributions? You should make it easy for employers to quickly scan through these by linking them in the README.

Github will give you a free URL that looks like "[yourname].github.io". It is fine to use that for your portfolio, but if you have purchased a personal domain like 'yourname.-com' then you can also point that to your Github page; then link your github portfolio page to your blog which will also be at the same domain (e.g. example.com/blog).

That is really all there is to it. You can always make adjustments as you go along and work on more projects and want to show off different skills.

~

TIP: Pay Attention to Your Github Profile

Keep in mind that it is not just your profile page that people will be looking at. Most companies will crawl through your Github account to see the projects you created and worked on. Make sure you are showcasing your best work front and center on your profile page. Also, if you have code that is not quite ready for anyone to look at, either remove it, set it to private, or add a note to the top of the README.md file that says the project is still under construction and is not in a usable state at the moment.

What to Include in Your Portfolio

Every time you add an app to your portfolio, you will want to take a clean screenshot that shows off what the app looks like while it is running. Do not take a picture of the code - it will neither look interesting nor be helpful to understanding what your app does. Include a link to the Github repository where they will be able to search through the code and understand it. Here is an example:

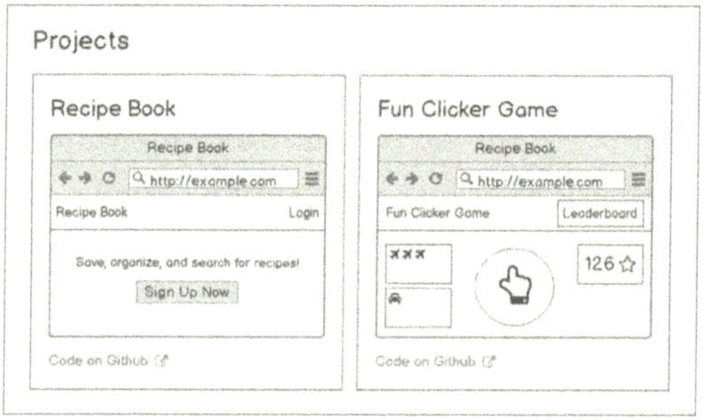

At first, your portfolio should include every app and website you build, including the most basic ones. After you have your first 5-6 projects completed, you can start to be more selective about which ones you want to show off.

As you are nearing job-readiness, you should start to consider polishing the apps that you are displaying on your portfolio. A few hours invested into making sure the interface looks clean and runs smoothly will return dividends when potential employers are reviewing what you built. It is also important to look at the code you wrote and make sure it is clean (e.g. remove any unnecessary code blocks, document how everything works in a README.md file, etc.).

Keep in mind that you do not want only boilerplate projects like to-do applications in your professional portfolio. Everyone learning to code builds one of these and you want to do your best to stand out among other applicants when you're applying for jobs. You should try to highlight a passion project that you have creatively envisioned and built. This will also help when they ask you about it in interviews because your passion will show. If you cannot think of anything creative or original to build, try re-creating a more complex application that you use regularly like a mail service (e.g. Gmail), crowdfunding platform, or marketplace (e.g. Ebay); then put your own spin on it. If you can build a complicated app like the ones I just mentioned, you will impress interviewers and anyone else looking at your portfolio.

It is also a good idea to include different types of apps in your portfolio. Do not use the same libraries, designs, and frameworks for everything. Try something new each time. Employers look for people who are adaptable and flexible, and your portfolio should showcase that ability.

Shoot for having at least one app in your portfolio where you collaborated on the code with someone else. This could be with your pair programming partner, an open source project, or an app you worked on with other people at a local meetup group. Make sure you have made several distinct contributions (commits) to the codebase. It is extremely important to show companies that you can work with other people and that you have already developed collaboration skills. Working with other people is something you would be doing almost everyday if you went to a coding bootcamp; you can easily get the same experience while learning on your own but you will have to facilitate those collaborations.

Conclusion

A current portfolio of the best apps you have built and what you are working on is extremely important to have when looking for your first job as a developer. Without actual work experience, most companies will not give you a second glance. You have to make them want to look and see that you have the right skills with a polished, professional portfolio.

Action Steps:

1. Perform an internet search for developer portfolios and take some notes about what you find.
2. Follow my guide to creating your own portfolio quickly at gwenfaraday.com/learn-to-code-book/portfolio.
3. If you have a personal domain, point it to your portfolio site.
4. Update your portfolio regularly and make sure you have a good variety of polished apps when you are looking for a job.

20

RÉSUMÉS

Even though you already have a portfolio, you still need to keep an up-to-date resume. Most HR departments require a standard text resume that can be saved in a format like Microsoft Word or PDF and kept on file. Your resume is also what many interviewers use to reference during interviews, and is required when you apply online to most positions.

When I was looking for my first job, my resume looked terrible and was utterly disorganized at first. I asked a few recruiters and developers look at it and suggest changes that I could make. I took their advice, made a lot of updates, and, after that, I noticed a difference in how many companies were calling me in for interviews.

This chapter will cover everything I have learned about developer resumes over the years; the kinds of information you should include on your resume as well as some other important details.

What to Include on Your Resume

As someone breaking into the industry, you will have to be a bit more creative than someone who can rely on their experience to get them in the door. On average, recruiters only take about 30-60 seconds to review a resume, so you should make important details stand out and keep the format scannable and easy to read.

To make resumes easier to read and digest, they are normally broken down into sections. Most resume experts, including the ones at Google and other tech companies, recommend a slightly different order and focus for software engineering applications: list the tools, languages, and frameworks that you know at the top, then work experience and education, and finally, volunteer experience, open-source contributions, and community involvement.

The order listed above is just a guideline and you might want to switch it up depending on your specific experience. For example, if you recently graduated college and you took classes relevant to software engineering, you could move education up to the top of your resume. Alternatively, if you are new to the industry and do not have relevant work experience yet, you might want to move your open source contributions or volunteer experience above the work section.

If you aren't a resume expert, creating a resume from scratch can be very time consuming. Use a resume template and replace the content with your own. I have a resume template template you can use linked from the content for this book on my website.

Here is a section-by-section breakdown of how you should organize your resume.

Name & Contact Information

This information should be at the very top and your name should stand out in slightly larger text than the rest of your resume. You do not need to list your full street address – email address, city, and state are enough. You should also include a link to your portfolio website, and, optionally, your blog and Github profile at the top below your name or other contact information.

About Me

Most employers do not require objective sections at the top - even though they are common. In fact, it is generally not recommended to write an objective section because they do not tell the interviewer much about you. Instead, you can opt to include a section with a snippet about yourself. After two or three sentences, you can include a link to a video or blog with more information about you. Recording a one to three minute video of yourself explaining your technical abilities and what you are looking for in your career can really help potential employers connect with you. It should take you no more than an hour or two to plan out your script, record the video, host it on YouTube, and include a link to it in your resume.

Skills & Knowledge

You should have bullet-pointed lists of the languages, tools, frameworks, and technologies that you know how to use. Include industry-standard professional tools like code editors in these lists so employers will see that you develop in the same environments you will use on the job.

Most people wonder when it is okay to list a skill on their resume. A good rule of thumb is you can include any technology that you have used to build something. If you utilized it on a project, add that to your resume. If you have watched a video or gone through a getting started tutorial, then you should not add it to your resume yet. You will only gain enough knowledge about a technology by building something with it yourself, not just following instructions.

Here are some examples of things you might want to include in this section:

- **Languages:** JavaScript, Python, Ruby, Go, HMTL5, CSS3, Sass
- **Frameworks & Libraries:** Vue.js, ReactJS/React Native, EmberJS, AngularJS, jQuery, Rails, Flask, Bootstrap, Lodash, Handlebars, PhoneGap
- **Skills and Knowledge:** Responsive Web Design, Programming Paradigms, Optimization and Security best practices, Salesforce/SFMC Platforms, OSX and Android Mobile Development
- **Tools:** VS Code, SublimeText, Git, Gulp, Webpack, Rollup, NPM, OSX/Linux, Vim
- **Web Technologies:** Node.js, PHP, Web Services (REST), AWS, Heroku, DynamoDB, SQL, MongoDB

At first, you will likely only have a few of these listed. You might start with HTML and JavaScript, then pick up jQuery, and then learn how to use Git and Github. Your skills will continue building from there and you will wind up with a few items in each of these categories. Do not worry about putting too many different technologies on your resume as it might look like you are stretched thin, especially if it is your first job.

Work Experience

If you are just starting out, you might not have any work experience relevant to a career in programming. This is probably the most difficult section to fill in on your resume. Here are some tips to make your work history stand out to hiring managers even if you do not have much, or any, experience in the industry.

Your work experience should be listed in reverse chronological order, with your most recent job at the top. Details about your position and accomplishments can be listed as bullet points underneath each employer. If your employment has been short-lived or it is a temporary job, you can just use one bullet point to list your responsibilities.

First, be sure to include anything technical you have done at previous jobs. Did you use a piece of software, fix IT problems around the office, or update the company blog? List all of these things, if applicable. Another option, if you are still at the company, is to offer to perform technical tasks right now. If the website needs updating, then offer to use your skills to help. When you do, list this item as the first bullet point under that employer. You need to highlight your technical work and any initiative that you took even though it wasn't your primary job.

Also include any problem solving and leadership experience. These are both very relevant to almost any career, but problem solving is especially relevant as a programmer. It is a big part of what you will be doing every day. If you have received awards or recognition, list those at the top underneath the company as well. This is arguably the section where you need to try to sell yourself the most.

Finally, include consulting work here if you have built websites for local companies. As I recommended earlier in the book, offer to create or update a website or application for a company. It could be your local pizza parlor that needs an online menu or a stay-at-home mom looking to start a photography business. If the company doesn't have money to pay you, offer your services in exchange for a gift card or free pizza. The experience is more valuable than the money. Once you build one project for someone else, you can add a section to your work experience about your private consulting business with a list of projects you have worked on bulleted underneath.

Education

If you went to college, include it. If not, that's fine, too. List any coding programs you have used for your learning, like freeCodeCamp or completing some other coding curriculum on or offline. If you attended some college, but didn't graduate, list the name of the school, the years attended, and your focus or major. You do not need to write specifically that you didn't graduate as that could look negative to someone reviewing your resume.

If you have earned coding certificates, list each one of those individually here. They may not hold much weight at the company you are applying to, but at least it will show that you are committed to your learning and personal development.

Volunteer & Community

This section demonstrates that you are active in the programming community and value giving back. Have you created or helped with a meetup group? Taught coding to kids? Volunteered for Doctors Without Borders or something non-tech related? List that experience here in short bullet points with the year(s) when you did the volunteer work. If you do not have any volunteer experience to list, I strongly suggest you start now. Sign up to volunteer for something like a local community cleanup group or teaching kids how to code at least once a month. This will make you feel good, make the interviewer feel good about you, and also give you something you are passionate about to bring up at the interview.

If you have given technical talks, written tutorials, contributed to open source, or made YouTube videos about coding, list all of those here as well. When you have multiple of any of these items, you can just use one bullet point for each category like so:

- **Event Speaker:** An In-depth Look at Regex, Functional Programming in JavaScript
- **Text Tutorials:** Getting Started with Python, Human-first Design in Vue.js
- **YouTube Videos:** How to Use Jupiter Notebooks Series, VS Code Shortcuts
- **Contributions:** Core Contributor, Regex Breakfast; Author, Vue Simplicity

Other Recommendations

- Do not include references. You can save your references for companies that request them and are serious about considering you for employment.
- Do not include the words junior or irrelevant, meaningless certifications like W3Schools

HTML certification (many sites have tests you can take online for 'certifications'; do not fall for it, they may just make you look more inexperienced). Use certifications from online programs that actually make you build something and have a good reputation like freeCodeCamp, Udacity, and The Odin Project.
- Do not use bar charts to show the percentage proficiency you have in a technology. There is no standard by which to compare the amount you have filled in the chart. If you have used/built something with a technology, then you can add it to your resume, just do not lie about your level of proficiency in an interview. Good tech interviewers will be able to tell your skill level just from talking with you for a few minutes.
- Check for typos and have someone proofread it. I have personally seen people rejected from positions for having typos because it comes across that you are not detail-oriented, or possibly that you don't care enough about the job (or your professional image) to take the time to proofread it. You want to put yourself in the best possible light, and if someone else's resume doesn't have typos, but yours does, the company may move another candidate forward instead of you.

Design & Style Tips

- Font should be readable and the same everywhere. Black or dark ink on a white background - high contrast - is best for readability.

- Use bullet points, not paragraphs.
- Do your best to fit your resume onto one page. Interviewers do not want to see unrelated content, so take the time to parse through your bullet points and only include what is relevant. When you get more experience, your resume will grow.
- Again, do not use progress bars. There is no objective measurement for what they mean.
- Most recent experience always goes first.
- Bullet points should be concise and clear.
- Resume experts recommend the use of action words like "created", "developed", "managed", etc. when you are writing the bullet points on your resume.
- Be sure to include the programming languages and tools you used for each project or at each company.

Order of Content

Jeremy Png, a technical recruiter for Google, recommends listing your programming languages at the top of your resume, above all of the other sections - in the header with your contact information. This makes it easy for employers to see what stacks you have experience working with.

The rest of the sections can be organized in the same order as I list them above - with the optional About Me section first, followed by Skills & Knowledge, and so on.

Cover Letters

From my experience, most programming jobs do not require an official cover letter. However, some companies (usually in industries like insurance or healthcare) will require you to include this with your resume. For other jobs, you may also have the opportunity to email your resume and you can make the email body your personalized cover letter.

I recommend creating a standard cover letter for yourself that you can modify slightly to personalize for specific companies (you should personalize it for every job you apply to). It should be one to two paragraphs long or a minimum of four sentences. You really want to use this space to connect and catch the attention of the person reading it. Share one or two sentences about your story and then talk about how you can help the company and why you fit in to the culture there.

Since you are new, be sure to emphasize that you are passionate about learning. This helps to show that you are humble and willing to adapt to their environment. Words are at a premium in your cover letter so be sure to go back over it several times and cut out any extra fluff.

Finally, do not forget to address it to the company and put your name on the bottom.

Conclusion

A resume is still the main document used to communicate your skillset to employers. Thus, it is important to put some extra effort into how you present yourself on your resume. Check out the related content for this book on my website for more information.

Action Steps:

1. Find a resume template.
2. Write out a draft of your resume and put it aside for a few days.
3. Review it again with fresh eyes and see if you can find ways to improve it.
4. Ask friends or some meetup acquaintances to review your resume and give you feedback.
5. Update your resume as you keep learning and according to the feedback you receive from job interviews.
6. Create a cover letter template that you can modify for different companies.

GETTING HIRED

Section 5

21

JOB OPPORTUNITIES

"Don't be wowed by HR and managers talking up the place — perfect companies do not exist! The best thing to do is write out the pros and cons for each company where you are entertaining employment opportunities. If you haven't found any cons yet, you haven't looked hard enough. There are problems in *every* company."

— GWENDOLYN FARADAY, AUTHOR

If you have started the job search already, you are probably wondering what kind of company you should work at when you are starting out and what type of job would best suit your needs. Throughout my career so far, I have worked at many different types of companies. From my experience, I can tell you one thing for sure: for your own happiness and career satisfaction, it is important that you understand the differences between company structures so you can choose one that aligns with your lifestyle and goals. This chapter will cover the main types of companies and positions you will encounter during your search for the right fit.

Note: this chapter covers developer jobs from the perspective of the United States market.

Location

It is important to determine how far you are willing to travel every day for work. If this is your first job, you may not be able to be as selective. When I started as a developer, I had to carpool 35 minutes every day to work. After I had some experience, I got to work at a company that was much closer to me.

In-Person

If you live within commuting distance of a city with at least a few hundred thousand people, there will be plenty of tech jobs available to you. This will make it much easier to find your first position.

I also recommend working in person for your first job. It is much easier to stay focused in an office and find help quickly when you need it. Most offices have quiet places for you to stow yourself away when you need deep focus, and the majority of tech companies have flexible working arrangements, so you may get to work from home a few days a week once you have been working there for a while.

Remote

It is rare, but not impossible, to find a remote job when you are starting out. Most companies do not want to take the risk on a brand new developer who will be working in isolation most of the time. It is much easier to train and mentor a new developer in person than over chat and occasional video calls. You might also feel lost having to work on your own right away.

If you cannot commute or need an extra flexible schedule, then yes, go for a remote job. Just know you will most likely have to work harder to get hired at one.

TIP: Relocating for Work

There are several reasons why you may want to consider relocating to find a job. If you live in a rural area that is far from any mid-sized or major cities, then you will have much better chances finding your first job if you relocate. As I mentioned above, it is already difficult to find a job as a junior, let alone a remote job. If relocating makes it even 25% easier, it might be worth it, especially if you do not have any obligations tying you to where you live.

You might also think about relocating if your past is an obstacle. Maybe you have received negative press about something you did in the past but do not identify with anymore. You could try to clean up your negative image both online and offline, but it might just be easier to move.

If you have a felony on your record, you will want to check on regulations and corporate sentiments in your area, and may even want to move to a friendlier place. I completely believe in hiring former felons who have been rehabilitated through the penal system, but some companies will not even give you a chance if you have a record.

Some companies offer relocation packages as part of their benefits package if they are trying to hire a candidate in a certain area. This offering can be rare for a junior developer, but if you are open to relocating to the area they are hiring in, it doesn't hurt to ask about it once you get to the final interviewing stages.

Characteristics of a Good Job

Chapter 21 will go over some questions you should ask to determine job fit, but here are some things to think about as you consider any position. As a new developer, your considerations will not only be benefits- and lifestyle-related, but whether the position will be beneficial to you and fit in with your long-term goals. Here is a list of the things you should consider when looking at job opportunities.

- Mentorship
- Ongoing training and education
- Growth opportunities
- Current onboarding process
- Current developer satisfaction (not just general employee satisfaction because how employees are treated can vary widely between departments at some companies)

TIP: Ignore the Fluff

Do not buy into the fluff that companies put on their blog, social media, and website. Dig into what it is really like to work there by networking and asking current and former employees. Read reviews on Glassdoor (take with a grain of salt) and other review websites if you can.

~

Other Tips & Recommendations

- Watch out for frequent changes in management: it could be that the company was bought out or has new upper management which would cause the company culture to change. There is usually high turnover when management changes and if it happens often, it is a good sign of much larger internal problems.
- Some companies are adamant about monitoring your time. I usually avoid these types of companies as they typically have overbearing leadership.
- There is nothing wrong with admitting something isn't working out, or you have learned all you can, and you need to move on.
- Create opportunities and internships for yourself. If no one will make space for you, then you have to do it, and it is usually not that hard. If you really want to work somewhere or just get experience anywhere, ask for an internship with a company! It doesn't matter if they aren't hiring. If you are able to work for a vastly reduced rate for a while, many smaller companies will be willing to take you on to get experience.
- You just need one job to say "yes", so keep

applying no matter how many times you get turned down.

TIP: When are you Ready to Start Applying for Jobs

There is no single point in time where you pass the ready threshold. Learning is a continuous process, so it is hard to say exactly when you are ready for a job, and even though you may feel unprepared, you need to start applying when you are not ready so that you can practice interviewing to prepare to be a serious candidate. I recommend that you start applying to jobs at around 400-500 hours of study if you are starting from scratch.

Conclusion

All of the details above are generalizations. Some companies do not fit into any mold. This advice is meant to give you a place to start. You will have to research each company individually to find out more about the specific working conditions and expectations. There are plenty of opportunities at each of the different company types. If you do not get your first pick right away, then keep it as a career goal for your second or third job in the industry.

Remember that applying for jobs is never a waste of time because you should be learning from every rejection. Your motto should be: keep applying, keep learning. I would love to hear about your experience in searching for the right position. Please let me know through email or Twitter, @faradayacademy.

Action Steps:

1. Decide which types of companies and positions you are most interested in.
2. Gear your job search towards them.
3. Set a goal for the number of job applications you will fill out each week.

22

RECRUITERS

"Engagement has to be human because people trust people more than brands."

— Ana Alonso, Global Marketing Head, Shell

Recruiters often get a bad rap in the tech industry even though they provide valuable services both to companies looking for talent, and to people trying to get noticed by those companies. Like most things in life, they are not all good or all bad—most of the time it depends on the person and how you interact with them. To make the most of your time, you should know what to expect.

This chapter will cover some basics on dealing with recruiters and give you some tips on making the most of your interactions with them.

What Recruiters Do

Recruiters do as their name suggests: they *recruit* people for positions. Sometimes they work internally for a company, other times they may work for themselves or specialized recruitment agencies that are hired by companies who need help filling jobs.

They are almost always paid through commission or on a bonus structure, particularly those who work for third-party staffing agencies who are not employed internally by the company. Rewards for placing programmers are remarkably high (averaging around $30,000 according to some estimates in the US market) compared to other industries, and successful recruiters could make a living off of placing just a few people per year. Sometimes this payment is a percentage of the candidate's salary over a period of time or just a lump sum.

It is important to remember that everyone has their own incentives and goals - the recruiters, the company, and the job seekers. No one should be blamed for doing what is in their best interest as long as they are being ethical and not intentionally harmful or deceitful. Even though the recruiter may try to sell you on a certain company or position, it's important to do your own investigative research apart from those interactions. During your job search, ensure that your incentives align with whatever company you ultimately get hired at.

During the hiring process, it is in the recruiter's best interest to treat you well and help you out, even if you are a beginner. You will one day be an experienced developer who can recommend that recruiter to your peers. Savvy recruiters know this and try to invest up front in the developer community to reap rewards later. These are the type of recruiters you want to network with.

How Recruiters Can Help You

Recruiters work for companies to fill recently vacated or new positions. In that pursuit, they can also be helpful resources for you in your job search.

Here are some ways that forming relationships with recruiters can be used to benefit you:

- **Reviewing resumes and cover letters:** Ask them to look over your resume and cover letter and take note of their recommendations. They are always trying to make resumes look more appealing to companies and review hundreds of resumes a week as part of their job, which gives them good insight into what a great resume is structured like and what skills hiring managers are looking for.
- **Career recommendations:** They can make career recommendations based on your goals. If you are looking for work-life balance, for example, they could recommend certain companies over others.
- **Networking:** Tech recruiters who have been in the industry for a while will usually have lots of connections in the area. If you establish a relationship with them, you can start asking them to make introductions for you with other well-connected people.
- **Interviews:** They can set you up with interviews as

part of their job. The best recruiters will also be able to set interview expectations with you and give you tips to help you prepare. It will be a bit harder to get interviews as a new programmer, even through a recruiter, but still not impossible. The market is short hundreds of thousands of programmers so they may be able to sell you to a company.

- **Support:** The recruiter you are working with should also be available to you throughout the interview process. You can ask them for recommendations or feedback as well as information about the company you are interviewing at.
- **Information:** Recruiters can give you information about the current and evolving job market. Third-party recruiting firms work with many different companies and applicants so they have a great view about what is going on in the tech market in your area.

If you want more information about how recruiters can help you, check out my podcast episode where I interview tech recruiter Nicole Osbun about this topic: faradaytechcafe.podbean.com/e/episode-12-understanding-developer-tech-recruiter-relationships-with-nicole-osbun.

Recruiter Strategy

Once you start listing tech experience on your LinkedIn profile, you will start being contacted by recruiters online. If you are proactive in your networking, you will be meeting local recruiters long before that happens, though. You need to prepare yourself for what to expect and how to get the most out of your interactions with recruiters.

First, you need to be sure you are working with the best recruiters for your situation. Most recruiters do not go to developer meetups which are normally held outside of business hours and require extra effort to attend. However, the ones who are really invested in the community, helping people, and networking - the savvy ones I mentioned earlier - will be going to these meetups. These are usually the best types of recruiters to connect with when you are getting started. Many of them are happy to meet you for coffee to look over your resume and chat about the tech industry. Take advantage of every opportunity you have with these types of recruiters to form relationships.

To get connected with more high-quality recruiters, ask for recommendations from lynchpins in the community, like meetup organizers or other well-connected individuals. Keep a list of them and reach out from time to time so you stay on their radar.

Even though many recruiters have never been programmers, the good ones research the technologies that they are trying to hire for. You have to know what you are talking about to some extent even with recruiters. If you are dishonest with them about your skills, it will come up in the interview process and you may get a bad name in the recruiter community where you live (they call it recruiter blacklisting).

When you start getting spammed by lots of recruiters online, remember that you do not have to reply. It is probably a good idea to accept any requests for recruiter connections on LinkedIn or other social media when you are starting out, but some recruiters lazily send out their messages to spam hundreds or thousands of people at the same time, hoping for replies from a few. Those messages or emails aren't personalized and often, the jobs requirements do not match your skills at all. Do not waste your time on pushy or low-effort recruiters. Only work with high quality ones who value your time and effort.

Questions for Recruiters

If you are going to work with a recruiter, you should interview them just like anyone else. Here are some ideas for questions to ask recruiters at your first meeting.

- What types of companies do you work with? *They will not tell you the names of the companies but you can ask for as many other details as you want as long as it does not give away too much.*
- What is your placement rate? *This will give you an idea of how effective the recruiter will be at placing you in a job.*
- What types of skillsets do you usually place for?
- What types of assessments do you think I will have to take for the companies I am looking at?
- What are you currently hiring for?
- What salary ranges do the people that you place typically receive?
- Where have you placed other candidates before? *They might not be able to tell you, but it is worth asking anyways.*

Other Tips & Recommendations

- You do not have to tell anyone how much money

you are making at your current job (it is actually illegal for companies to inquire about this during the application process in California). If it is your first job, you can do some research to get an idea of what companies will pay and then let them know an amount you are comfortable with.

- Be professional - it does not matter what you have heard people say about recruiters, they are just people doing their job and deserve the same respect as anyone else. Do not burn bridges and be polite in your interactions with them.
- It is okay to work with multiple recruiters. You are not cheating on one by working with another. In fact, you *should* be working with more than one. The only exception is recruiters working for the same recruitment firm. They will not be allowed to speak with you if you are already working with one of their coworkers.
- There are recruiters that you can hire who will work to find you a job. I recommend not spending the money on that unless you feel like you really need help. You really have to go through the experience of networking and job hunting on your own to get the connections you are going to need to grow in the industry.
- You have to be somewhat flexible. Recruiters are balancing many clients and applicants, and they may not get back to you right away. Do not feel bad about sending them reminder messages either. In my experience, they appreciate the reminder.
- Make sure they do not update your resume without your permission. You own your resume

and information. If they work for a company with scruples, this should not be a problem, but it cannot hurt to ask and make sure.

Conclusion

Recruiters can be valuable allies if you connect with the right ones. Go out there, network, and connect with as many well-connected recruiters as you can right now.

Action Steps:

1. Start connecting with recruiters in your community.
2. Ask around to get recommendations for the best recruiters to work with.
3. Meet with recruiters and solicit help with your resume and navigating the job market.
4. Make a list of recruiters you have connected with and stay on their radar by reaching out from time to time.

23

FINDING JOBS ONLINE

> "[T]he online job search (OJS), which was used by less than a quarter of all jobseekers at the turn of the century, is now the most popular method of job hunting."
>
> — Richard Hernandez, Author, U.S. Bureau of Labor Statistics

Internet job boards have been around for decades, and you have likely heard of some of the more popular ones like Indeed, Monster, and Career Builder. You can find posts for thousands of new tech jobs every month on these sites; not to mention lists of open positions on company websites and in random social media posts. The question is which ones are worth your time and effort? The answer to this question isn't black and white.

The success of your online job search depends on what strategy you use. In this chapter, we will learn about the types of places to find online jobs and how to strategize to make the most of your search.

Where to Find Jobs

Job boards

This is the most common place your mind will go when you hear about online jobs. There are hundreds of these sites in three main categories: general ones with every type of position represented, programming-specific ones with different types of software engineering roles (and sometimes supporting roles at tech companies), and niche boards that target people in a specific area of tech or type of work, such as web development or remote positions.

I recommend avoiding generalized job boards like Indeed, Monster, or Career Builder. The positions posted in these places have a lot of applicants applying to them every day, increasing the likelihood that you will not stand out as a new developer. You will also get screened twice, likely by automated software both times (once from the job board site, and once by the company looking to weed out most of the applications they receive before they have a human look at the remaining ones). You should not fault companies for doing this. They have to be profitable and it is a waste of money to filter through thousands of applications for one open position. Be smart and reach these companies through the other methods I mention in this chapter.

Then there are tech-only job sites like techjobs.com. Most of the positions listed on these sites will be too advanced for your skillset. In the event that that there are entry-level job listings, they will receive numerous applications. I would recommend you do not spend your time applying on these sites right now.

If you know you want to work in a specific type of

coding, location, or environment, try to find niche job boards for it and look at what kind of jobs are listed there. Most of these jobs will be too advanced for your skillset, but you can find some great job opportunities on these sites. There is usually less screening on these job boards and much less competition.

One thing that you might find on any of these sites is automated filtering, also called auto-rejecting. Auto-rejecting means that a computer program is set up to reject resumes that do not meet certain criteria, so the hiring manager or HR may never see your resume at all. For example, sites like Indeed will let you fill out and submit a whole application, but if you do not say you have experience in one of the required fields, they will never forward your application to the company.

One more important piece of advice: Do not upload your resume on these job boards. You mostly get a lot of annoying spam and it is almost always a waste of time.

Company websites

If you have worked through the action steps I go over in this book, you should have already decided on the types of jobs and companies that will be able to meet your career needs. You will now be able to make lists of companies in your area, find their websites, look at what jobs they have open, and apply through their company-specific portal. This is much better than applying on generalized job boards because there will be less screening and competition. Applying directly makes it look like you want to work specifically with that company instead of just randomly finding the company.

If you do see a job you want to apply for on a job board,

double check the company's website to see if they have posted the same thing there. Large companies in particular will usually cross-post open positions in multiple places.

Professional Websites

These professional sites, like LinkedIn, also list jobs directly on their platform and are probably your best bet to getting hired online. The great thing about this type of site is that when you find a company where you want to work, you will be able to see the employees that work there along with everyone's position or title. I advise looking on LinkedIn specifically for all of the companies and positions you want to apply for.

You should connect with both engineers and recruiters at every relevant company that you can. Ask them in a message for help with getting to know the needs of their company. Tell them that you really want to apply for a job and ask them if they have advice on what the company is looking for and how to stand out. Most people want to be helpful and will be happy to answer your question if you approach them in a friendly way. If they live in your area, offer to take them out for a coffee in a location that is convenient to them. Chat with them about the culture and what it is like to work at the company. You never know, if you stand out to them in person, they might even recommend you for the job so they can get a referral bonus. More details on connecting with other professionals can be found in Chapter 11.

Social Media

Social media is also a great place for finding jobs and

connecting with companies. You can easily find employees - on Twitter especially - from these companies you want to work at along with accounts from the companies themselves. As you are already building your social media presence, why not interact with companies directly on these platforms?

If you follow companies and their employees, you may see them tweet out job openings that might not even be posted online yet. That is your chance to reply to the post and say that you are interested and are going to apply. Doing this will get the company to notice you and may give you a leg up with getting an initial interview.

Strategy for Getting Callbacks

Outside of a generic "thank you for applying" confirmation email, you may not receive word from the company that anyone has reviewed your resume for quite some time. If you apply through an online job portal, you may be able to log back in and view the status of your application, but generally applying for jobs takes a lot of patience.

You have to be very strategic to get a callback when you do not have development experience. Here are some tips to help.

What To Avoid

Whatever you do, do not resume spray! This means do not apply to lots of companies at once using the same resume and information. This will get you nowhere except maybe with low-caliber companies that will give you the run-around. It is also a good way to apply to fake jobs and get your email, name, and phone number collected by spammers.

You will also find lots of companies online that have unreasonable expectations. Here are some examples:

- Companies asking for multiple years of experience but still calling the position "junior" or "internship". This makes them come off as cheap and out of touch.
- Companies that are asking you to do too many things like knowing three or more different programming languages or doing design and front-end and back-end and customer service, etc.
- Companies that post an unreasonable salary range for the type of job. You can easily find both national average ranges as well as how much employees in your area can expect to make. If a company is offering to pay you well below that range, move on to the next application.

Run away from companies like these. They will just waste your time that you could be using to apply at companies that will respect you and help you grow.

When to Apply

While there are studies that show that if an applicant doesn't meet 90-100% of the criteria in an online job posting, they will not even be considered for the position, this doesn't apply quite as much in tech. This is partly because of the overwhelming demand for software engineers, and partly because, many times, the people writing the job descriptions do not understand the technology.

There is nothing wrong with applying for lower-paying jobs like internships or junior developer positions if it is temporary or there is a path for you to move up from there. I would say if you are motivated, it should take between six months and a year to move past the junior level into a mid-level position.

It is completely okay to apply for jobs even if you do not meet all of the requirements, the truth is, you will probably have to in order to get hired. I have seen many job postings that require two or more years of experience be filled with entry-level developers. Do not lie about your experience, but do not be afraid to try to land a job that is advertised as beyond your current skill level as long as it is in the same kind of software development that you have already been studying, like mobile or web development. I would not recommend going outside of your area of study if you do not have to in the beginning because it can cause a lot more work and additional stress.

You can also try to give yourself a leg up by applying to a job early in the morning (before 7 am). Some studies suggest that you are far more likely to get an interview if you submit the application at that time. Personally, I have never tried this time-based method, but it is an interesting idea if you want to give yourself an additional advantage.

How to Apply

The applications you submit should be customized to every employer. You will have to do some research and, most importantly, carefully read the whole job description. If they want you to apply via email then make sure you include the different pieces of your cover letter in your email, plus a few sentences touching upon specifics of the company and job requirements to let them know that you did your research. Make sure you attach your resume. I have forgotten to attach my resume with several email applications in the past so make sure you double check everything before you hit send.

If it is a job application portal, scroll through all of the answers you need to respond to first and write them out in another place like a digital notepad. Then paste them into the application when you are done. You have no idea if you will be able to view those answers later and you can reuse them for future applications.

There are also more creative ways to apply to these jobs online. If the company only has their open positions posted on job boards, you can try to contact the company directly and say you would like some help applying and ask for HR's or the hiring manager's contact info. Then you can reach out to that person directly and skip the line, so to speak.

Following up

Keep a list of all the places you have applied to and the dates that you submitted the applications. If you haven't heard back from a company within about a week, you should send them an email or message to check on the status of your application. Do not worry about being bothersome. They posted a job and should expect to be contacted about it.

I got hired at one company I had applied to online because I was very persistent with the owner and manager until they gave me a shot; I probably sent them between eight and ten reminder emails. I ended up working there for almost two years and had a great time. I do not recommend 'bothering' anyone that much, but it doesn't hurt to send a few reminder emails to get your resume dug out of the pile and probably reviewed more quickly.

Set a goal

Set a goal to apply to at least 3-5 places every week in addition to the in-person networking you are doing. You can either batch them all at once or try to do one per day. I personally like batching them once per week so I do not have to remember to do one every day.

Creating your Own Opportunities

There are a lot of companies that are always looking for the right people, even if they do not have any job openings posted. I recommend inserting yourself into these roles by contacting the company, telling them how interested you are, and trying to set up a chat with whoever does the hiring, even if it is just a quick phone call. Ask them to give you a shot, maybe an internship or another working arrangement to see how you work. They may like your boldness and figure they might just be hiring their next good engineer for a steal.

One time, at the end of a second-round interview I had with a company I really wanted to work for, I asked them to just let me spend two days with their employees to see if it was a good match. They agreed, so I worked for two days and they liked me so much that they hired me after that. I do not think I would have been hired for that job if I had just let that second interview end with the usual, "You will receive an email from us within the next few days."

Be bold. Ask for what you want. If you do not get the job, you can just move on to the next company.

Other Tips & Recommendations

- I really want to hammer this into your head: Use spelling and grammar checks. Make sure every message you send has been double-checked before you hit the submit button. You want to give yourself the best shot at every opportunity by being very polished.
- Fill out every field in the job application to make sure you are not auto-rejected.
- I didn't talk about jobs on sites like Quora and Stack Overflow here because it is very difficult to get jobs on these and I do not think it is worth your time right now.
- Do not put your desired salary in an application. If there is a field that asks for that, I would suggest writing "Negotiable" or 0 if the field requires a number.

Conclusion

You can absolutely get hired online but you have to have a strategy so you aren't squandering your time and energy. If you stick to your goals, keep applying, and network consistently, you will start getting callbacks and interviews out of your applications.

Action Steps:

1. Based on how much time you have available, make a goal for how many applications you want to submit every week. Set aside time on your calendar when you will fill them out.
2. Make a list of the companies you want to apply at and connect with employees who work there.
3. Ask their employees for help in standing out in the application process.
4. Do your research on the company and carefully read the job posting, if there is one, before applying.
5. Customize the application.
6. Follow up with the company after one week. If they do not respond to your follow-up, then continue to follow up every week after that until you get an official ”yes” or ”no” on your application.

24

INTERVIEWING

We could spend a whole book talking about interviewing, but I'm going to boil it down to the basics of what you need to know to get started right now. I include more information in the resources for my book.

Interviewing is a process and involves more than simply answering questions and waiting for a phone call. You will probably have to go through many interviews with many different companies. Do not worry, most people, even if they have experience, will bomb interviews sometimes. The trick is to just be honest about what you know with the interviewers, make a connection with them, try to get feedback, and learn something every time.

Types of Interviews

On average, programming jobs will have three rounds of interviews: an initial interview with the hiring manager or recruiter where they will ask you standard interview questions, then a technical interview to make sure you can do the job, and, finally, an interview with the team to ensure that you are the right fit for the culture at the company. Some companies will have more rounds than this, but additional interview rounds are usually for additional employees or managers to meet you and they will probably ask you the same kind of questions I list here.

General Question Interviews

These interviews typically consist of one or two interviewers asking you standard interview questions. The company uses this time to weed out candidates that are obviously a bad fit or have poor interpersonal skills. At this stage, they probably will not ask too many in-depth technical questions, but you can expect more generalized questions about why you want to get in the field and what you have built or accomplished so far.

Technical Interviews

This is the most difficult type of interview and the one that everyone gets nervous about. Every company does this a little different: some will make you pair program with other people on the team, some will make you solve problems on a whiteboard, and some will drill you with deep technical questions. You also might get some combination of these three.

When you make it to the technical interview, the company should let you know the details about what they are going to ask you to do.

Culture Fit Interviews

This is where you will probably meet the whole team and answer questions from other developers and team leaders. You can also ask them questions about what it is really like to work at the company. By the time you are at this interview, the company is already considering you to be a serious candidate for the position. The goal here is to be friendly and humble with the team. Make sure they see that you are able to handle criticism well and work as a part of a team.

Off-Site Interviews

Sometimes companies will invite you to lunch or coffee for an interview. I have seen this a lot with consulting companies who want to see how you present yourself and interact with other people, not just the interviewer that you are trying to impress. You should prepare by researching the venue and their menu. It is a good idea to know what you are going to order before you arrive. Try not to be picky and be kind to the people that are serving you. The interviewer will take note of every interaction you have.

Phone Interviews

Many companies will schedule a brief phone screening before the first interview. These are usually mid-sized or smaller companies who want to whittle down the field more efficiently than through in-person interviews. You should try to ask questions that build a relationship with the interviewer, which will show them that you are well-prepared and interested in the role

If you are applying for remote companies, you will probably be doing only phone interviews and video conferences via Skype or Zoom. Make sure you read over the instructions ahead of time and download whatever video conferencing technology they are asking you to use. Make it a point to join the call five minutes early and wait for other participants. Even though it may not be as formal as an in-personinterview, tardiness will not be easily forgotten by the interviewers. You should always use headphones on these calls to cut out background noise and distractions, and make sure you look clean and presentable.

Companies will also usually call you in between each round of interviews but these calls are just to give you information and set expectations. Make sure you ask them questions about next steps if anything is unclear. Be polite and thank them each time.

Interview Preparation

The more prepared you are before the interview, the more impressive you will look to the company. It shows that you are organized and driven, and every company wants to hire eager and motivated people. As a beginner, and especially if you are self-taught, it is going to be difficult for you to get noticed by companies. The best way to give yourself an advantage is with thorough preparation.

Interview preparation starts with doing research about the company:

- Look at their website and social profiles.
- Learn about their mission and what they do.
- If they have software products that you can access, download them and test them out.
- Look into any open source projects they contribute to.

Additionally, reach out to former and current employees about their experience at the company. You will often find that employees will give you important nuggets of information on what you might experience in the interview process. One example is a recruiter who worked for a company I was interviewing at let me know that my interviewer really liked the book *Clean Code* by Robert C. Martin. I made sure to reread the book and brought it up during the interview. The interviewer was impressed and we formed a great connection right away.

During your research, you will probably stumble upon employee reviews on sites like Glassdoor. Take these with a grain of salt. They are usually written by disgruntled employees or, in the case of the positive ones, people asked to write reviews by the HR department or management. Some of them are real, but it is usually hard to tell unless you speak with current and former employees from the department you will be working in.

Preparing questions

The standard practice in an interview is for the interviewer to ask if you have any questions for them before ending the interview. Employers will be concerned if you do not have any questions to ask or just have the low-effort ones like "What would I be doing in this role?" that you come up with off the top of your head. You should prepare the questions you are going to ask in advance.

You should ask questions that show you want to be successful if you take a job at this company. You also want to build a relationship with the interviewer and help them see you as a future coworker.

Here are some examples of good questions you can ask in general interviews:

- How did you come to work here? *Asking the interviewer these types of questions can help you build a relationship.*
- What do you like about working here? *This is a great question to ask for deciding if the company is the right fit for you.*
- What are your top company values?
- What is your policy about open source?
- What is the company policy on working on other projects outside of work? *This is a good question especially if you are planning on freelancing while you work at the company. Some companies do not allow you to do any kind of programming for pay outside of work. Just be careful that you do not come across as someone who does a lot of moonlighting; they might think that you won't have the mental energy or focus to fulfill your job responsibilities.*
- What are your policies on running a personal blog or making technical videos? *Very few companies have policies against these activities, but it is good to get information on what you can or cannot do up front so you do not make mistakes later.*
- What struggles are the company currently facing and how are you dealing with them?
- What challenges are you expecting to face in the future as the market evolves and how are you preparing for them?
- What challenges do some of the other developers experience here?

- Is there a good relationship between the IT department and the rest of the business?
- What additional skills do you think I need to learn first if I come on board at this company? *As a new developer, this is a good question to show that you are humble. It also gives you the chance to tell them that you have some experience in that area if they are mistaken, or to tell them that you will work on improving in that area.*
- Is there any reason you are hesitating in hiring me for the position? *This question can also show them that you handle feedback well.*
- Can I speak with one of the developers one-on-one? *If they say no to this question, you should question whether working at that company is the right choice. The only reason to not let you speak directly with a member of the team would be if they are hiding something; probably employee dissatisfaction. It is also ok to ask to talk to someone you can connect with. For example, I usually ask to talk to a female employee before I start working at a new job. It is just something that makes me feel more comfortable.*

Here are the questions you should be asking during interviews with the technical employees:

- How do you manage your projects?
- Do you work in sprints? What does a sprint look like? What sprint ceremonies do you perform?
- What does the development process look like?
- How long do developers normally stay at your company? Why do(n't) they stay?

- How does the team get along? If I asked any of the team members, would they have concerns about the cohesiveness of the team?
- When there is a problem, how is it addressed?
- What is the work-life balance like? How many hours do employees usually work? Overtime?
- Are there opportunities for me to be mentored and learn from senior developers? (Especially important if this is your first developer role.)
- What kinds of ongoing training opportunities do you provide?
- Can I speak privately with at least one developer on the team?
- Ask them some questions related to their tech stack based off of the research that you have done.

Prepare plenty of questions so you will have some left at the end when they ask you if you have any more questions. I like to pull out a notebook or tablet where I have my questions listed out to show the interviewer that I came prepared. If it is a remote interview, I also take lots of notes during the interview. You can also ask about what the next steps are, but the interviewer will usually cover that.

Preparing answers

There are several dozen common questions that you will be asked during a standard interview. You should write out the answers to these and practice saying them out loud before the interview. It even helps to watch yourself answer those questions in the mirror or record a video of yourself answering them so you can watch your facial expressions and tone and adjust them accordingly. Practice saying the answers with a smile and confidence, even if you are the only one in the room, it will help calm your nerves and feel more prepared for when you're in an interview.

The first category consists of open-ended questions. These are also the hardest to prepare for because they often have slight variations. You will almost always be asked the following:

- Tell me a little about yourself. *they want to see what is important in your background. Do not start talking about your childhood or anything else that happened a long time ago unless it is short and relevant. Focus on what led you to look for a job as a programmer.*
- Why do you want to work as a software developer?
- What made you interested in applying for this job?
- What do you like about this company?
- Tell me about a time when you ____.
- What would you have done in ____ situation?
- Give me an example where you displayed leadership or went above and beyond at a company.
- What would your previous co-workers say about you?
- What is your greatest weakness? *You should not say something positive like "I work too hard, it makes you sound disingenuous. Everyone has weaknesses or improvements they are working on professionally. Bring up an actual weakness and then tell them how you have been working to overcome that weakness. I*

always bring up my poor communication skills and how I have been working to improve them over the last decade.

- What are your strengths? Or, what is your greatest strength?
- What kind of salary/compensation are you looking for? *The salary question is tricky to answer. They should not be asking you about it until after the technical interview but it never hurts to be prepared up front. Do not give away the salary you are looking for in the first interview. Tell them that if we both feel like this job is right for me, then I'm sure we can come to an agreement that will make both of us happy. If it is the final interview and you are asked, then know what your value is and be able to support your value. Also, make sure you know what kind of total package you are looking for and not just salary.*

Any cut and dry questions such as, "What are your hobbies?" or "Where did you go to school?" should be easy enough to answer without practice. If you can prepare answers for the questions listed above, you will be starting off in a good place.

Preparing for Technical Interviews

Once you start getting companies asking you to interview with them, you need to start preparing for technical interviews. Your preparation steps should include algorithm challenges, pair programming, and learning about the latest updates of the technologies that you use. I recommend using HackerRank, Project Euler, freeCodeCamp, and Coderbyte. Try all of these platforms and pick one or two to use for your training. Do not be afraid of the word 'algorithm' either. You do not have to be a math wiz. The challenges start off from the very basics and get increasingly more difficult. You should plan to spend a few hours every week just working on these types of challenges to get your chops ready. When you feel comfortable doing the basic algorithm challenges on these sites, I also recommend that you take a look at Khan Academy's course on algorithms under their Computer Science curriculum. This will help you understand the best approaches for solving these problems.

At your level, you should expect to be given beginner or intermediate challenges in a technical interview. If they throw something advanced at you, they are probably not expecting you to be able to solve it, but rather seeing how you think. You should research the company's tech stack enough to be able to talk about it in the interview. When it comes to solving challenges, however, many companies will let you solve challenges in the language you know best, not just the ones they use.

If they ask you to whiteboard a solution, then you will be expected to write out your steps and talk them through it as you go along. It is difficult to write code with a marker, instead of a keyboard, not to mention explaining everything you are doing along the way. Some companies have told me that they do not care if you answer the problem fully, they just want to see your thought process, so that is what you should practice for.

There is a really good book called, *Cracking the Coding Interview* by Gayle McDowell that details how to handle these types of interviews. Many people will probably recommend it to you. I do think it is more advanced than you need when you are getting your first job in the industry. I recommend starting with doing some research on whiteboarding interview examples on YouTube and your regular search engine.

Pair programming interviews are getting increasingly more common. They are in many ways a more accurate measure of what you can do as a candidate because they are seeing you code live in your regular development environment. The best ways to prepare for these are to practice the algorithm challenges I mentioned earlier and practice pair programming with a partner as much as you can. Again, they are not just looking for correct solutions in these interviews; they want to see how you solve problems on the fly and how you work with other people.

During the Interview

The number one best thing you can do for yourself is to be relaxed and act natural. More important than technical ability is how the people in the company perceive you during the interview process. Take a deep breath and walk in with a smile. What's the worst thing that can happen? If you do not get the job, there will be plenty more opportunities for you.

Even in the tech world, soft skills are important. Be friendly and likable. A 2019 LinkedIn Global Trends survey found that soft skills was, by far, the number one job skill that companies look for. Lydia Liu, Head of HR at Home Credit Consumer Finance Co., said "While hard skills may get a candidate's foot in the door, it is soft skills that ultimately open it."

Have a notebook or tablet ready to jot down quick notes and to reference the list of questions that you have prepared to ask the interviewer, but do not spend too much time looking down at your notes. Making eye contact and connecting with the interviewer is important.

During the interview, you should make sure to bring up what you are passionate about even if it is not tech-related. This will help the interviewer connect with you. You also have to show them what makes you valuable and what you plan to accomplish in this new role. These are all things that you should be thinking of how to insert into your answers during the interview.

If you get bogged down thinking that they will not want you because of your lack of experience, you likely won't get past the first interview. You have to assume that you are qualified for the job and that you are an exceptional candidate. They are interested in you because they invited you for an interview, so use that knowledge to give you some confidence going in.

Illegal Questions

Discrimination in a job interview is illegal (I am speaking about the U.S. regulations here, you will have to look up your local laws if you live in another country). Do not answer questions related to age, sex, home ownership, place of origin, ethnicity, race, or religion. That stuff doesn't matter in a professional job interview. Sometimes they try to ask these questions in a roundabout way, and if you feel weird about a question, say that you want a moment to think about it first. Before the interview, do some research about what questions the interviewer is not allowed to ask and make sure you do not offer up that information either.

There are also questions that should not be asked, even if they are not illegal (in a few states they are illegal). These include asking a woman if she is pregnant or plans to become pregnant, or about her childcare situation. Do not expose personal information like this. Unfortunately, it may open the door for job discrimination, especially in tech where it can be demanding to keep up with new technologies. If they think you might be taking months off of work soon to have a baby, then you might not get the job for reasons that have nothing to do with fit or qualification.

Take-Home Projects

This is a very common part of the interview process. A company will ask you to build a small application or feature according to a set of instructions. You will usually have about a week to complete the assignment and upload it to Github or wherever else they want.

I recommend not spending more than 5-10 hours on this type of project. Yes, it is a learning experience and good to impress them, but you are not getting paid for your time either. If you do not finish all the features that they wanted you to, note that in the email that you send them when you are done with the project. Most of the time, they are not expecting you to finish everything. They want to see how you write code and prioritize your work.

Following Up

Writing them a thank you note within 24 hours of the interview is basic etiquette. It just has to be a few sentences expressing your gratitude and saying that you look forward to hearing from them soon. It is also nice to include some new information that you learned from the interview.

Wait a week and you can send them another follow-up email or message if they haven't contacted you yet. Sometimes, they just get busy and forget, so it is good to remind them that you are still interested.

If you get a rejection email, then reply graciously, say that you want to improve, and ask for feedback. Some companies have policies against giving you any information on why they aren't going to hire you, but some companies or employees you met with will be more than happy to give you insight into how they think you can improve.

Other Tips & Recommendations

- Do not bring up salary with a company until the very end when they know your worth. Research current industry salaries at places like Salary.com. I keep saying this throughout the book, just to make sure you remember when you are asked on the spot for this number.
- The only time you should bring up salary early is with a third-party recruiter.
- Make sure you never tell interviewers what you are currently making.
- Honesty and showing that you can learn from mistakes is important.
- Many companies want likable, presentable people. Especially if you are client-facing. I have read about other companies that will not hire people who show up in a suit. Know your audience and dress slightly better than the rest of people: if it is a casual place where the developers wear T-shirts, then show up in a polo. If it is a consulting job, then you might be client-facing so

you should show up wearing a suit if possible. Do not feel bad about asking the recruiter how people at the company normally dress.

- Do not be too informal in your manner of speaking either. They are not your friends; you are there to establish a working relationship.
- Do not overshare. No one needs to hear your life story when they have just met you.
- Do not sound overqualified. Go in knowing as much as you can about what they want and what you want.
- Do not be boring. Act interested in what the company is doing.
- Be forward. Ask them to try you out. This has worked for me in the past. Like I said earlier in the book, create your own opportunities.
- Be able to talk about why the company fits in with what you want and also how you can fit in and help the company.
- Use the word ”we” in the interview when talking about previous employers. This makes you sound like a team player.
- Practice with someone. Sometimes you do not realize what mistakes you are making.
- Have some enthusiasm about the technologies you work with.
- Show enthusiasm about the opportunity at the company, not desperation. Do not say, “I really need this job.” Say, “I'm excited about this position.”
- Do not second guess your answers or bring up that you are nervous.

- Do not say bad things about the company or product.
- Do not say bad things about previous employers or managers. If they ask about a previous company that you were let go from, just say that there were value or cultural differences between you and the company or managers.
- Be punctual. Make sure you save their number in your phone in case something happens and you have to be late. Being prepared the night before usually prevents this situation. I very embarrassingly was late to an interview four minutes from my house because I couldn't find the coffee shop and I didn't have the interviewer's number saved. I felt flustered for the whole interview after that.
- Show them that you have a positive attitude about work and life.
- Do not be arrogant. Pretending that you are perfect is a big mistake. You do not know everything.

Conclusion

Interviewing is a way to build a relationship with current employees at the company and for you to see if it is a good fit for you. If you are adequately prepared and keep interviewing at more companies, then you should have no problem getting through the rounds and receiving offer letters.

Have you had an experience interviewing that you would like to share? Let me know on Twitter, @faradayacademy, or by emailing contact@faradayacademy.com.

Action Steps:

1. Start practicing algorithms and pair programming for the technical interview.
2. Write down answers to all of the most common questions and practice them over and over until they feel natural.
3. Make a list of questions for you to ask companies. Customize this list slightly for every interview.
4. Review things that went well or poorly after every interview and try to improve.

25

JOB OFFERS

You are going to be ecstatic when you start receiving job offers. Try to tame your excitement for a moment, you are not out of the woods yet. You still might need to go through a negotiation process. You might also decide that the job is not a good fit for you when you read the fine print.

Remember that as a new developer, you may have to take a job that is not ideal for the long-term, but it should still meet your survival needs and allow you to grow. Your baseline goal for your first job should be a stepping stone to where you want to get in your career. Do not just take a job because it is the only thing that comes along. Be strategic about what is going to help you long-term in your career.

Receiving Job Offers

Review the job offer carefully and see how it stacks up to what you really want. Most companies like to tout that they give you lots of vacation or a good salary, but hide the areas they are weak in like health insurance or retirement options.

You have to separate needs from wants and decide where your line is.

Do not feel like you have to respond right away to a job offer. You can thank them right away and tell them you will get back to them by the end of the week or after the weekend (about 3-5 days from the date of the offer). Make sure you have a clear head when you are making decisions about where you will work for months or years.

What do you do if the offer does not meet your needs or you think it undervalues your work? Do not get upset or dismissive. First, try to be rational and negotiate before you shoot down the offer. Negotiating has helped me get much better packages at companies several times in the past.

Negotiating

To put yourself in the best negotiating position, Linda Raynier, a career coach and recruitment expert, advises that when the company asks you for your salary requirements to, "Give a number, not a range" Companies almost always go for the lowest end if you give them a range. It also makes you look unsure of what you want if you give a range. She recommends giving the employer your ideal number, slightly higher than what you would expect to actually receive. You would be thrilled to really get that number, but you should also have a fallback "willing to settle number" that is more in line with what entry-level developers make in your area.

Never get upset during negotiations, this is the most important time to stay level-headed so you can position yourself in the best situation possible while maintaining your composure and being respectful. Margaret Neale, professor of management at Stanford, said, "Folks typically see negotiation as an adversarial process and they are uncomfortable because they're concerned that other folks will think of them as too demanding, too greedy, not nice, or socially awkward." She advises changing your mindset about negotiations from an adversarial process to one that is problem solving. If you become flustered or disrespectful during the negotiation process, the company may decide they don't want to hire you based on your actions and can rescind your offer.

During the negotiation stage, you are simply trying to come to an agreement with the company on what your time is worth. If you are underpaid, you will not be happy or, even worse, be able to live comfortably, which will distract you from your work. If you are overpaid by too much, then the company might have unreasonable exceptions of you. You might have to be a little flexible but do not take less than your "willing to settle" number. I do not want you to get taken advantage of, like many new tech workers are. If you live in the United States, I recommend not taking a job at a large company for less than $50,000 per year or at a smaller company for less than $40,000 per year. That is the absolute minimum you should be receiving unless you are going to be working part-time. You might need to be making more than that if you live in a major metropolitan area where the cost of living is higher. If you take a low salary to start that you can live on, the best way to get a raise is by switching jobs after the first year because, unfortunately, many companies will fight to not give you raises to bring you up to market value.

To negotiate a higher salary, be sure to talk about your value. Remind them of how you performed in the technical interview, about your achievements and accomplishments. Show them how you have shown leadership, dedication, and hard work in the past. Another good idea is to use leverage for getting the salary you want. Tell the company that you have received multiple offers that you are considering. I did this before and got two of the three companies to offer me a lot more than I asked for.

Finally, before you contact the company, weigh the benefits versus the costs of negotiating. Make sure you have clear answers for what you are trying to achieve as well as what the company will think is reasonable.

When you go to write the email or prepare something to say over the phone, be sure to thank them first. Then let them know that you want to come to an agreement that is satisfactory to both you and the company, and remind them of your value. If they offered you below the industry standard for your experience and locale, then politely let them know about that. Then, tell them the number you want and ask them how they can help you work out a deal that makes sense for both of you. If you have a solution that you think they will find reasonable, pitch it to them.

You should also consider negotiating for other benefits besides compensation. If the salary is lower than market value, you can ask them to give you a transportation stipend, reimbursement for education opportunities, work from home days, flexible hours, or anything else on your ”wants” list.

A reminder for women: Studies show that women are uncomfortable asking for more money and do not negotiate nearly as often as men. Employers will almost never give you more than you demand. I recommend looking up Sheryl Sandberg's negotiating advice for women and practicing your negotiation techniques. It is a skill just like coding and it will help you in many more areas than just job offers

Common Problems

Sometimes negotiations fail and the company declines your counteroffer. It might be for budgetary reasons or something else entirely. Ask them if they will be open to renegotiating after you prove yourself at the company. Try to get them to commit to revisiting your salary after six months of employment and get it in writing.

The company may draw a line in the sand and say they will not or cannot give you what you want. That is not the optimistic result, but there is not much else you can do at that point. You will have to choose if that is acceptable, or if you want to part ways and continue job searching.

If the numbers are lower than you expected, try negotiating as I said above. This is a common problem for new developers. If they are significantly low, then I would question if the company is legitimate or worth your time at all.

Accepting a Job Offer

Do it over the phone or in person. If they extend the offer to you via email, ask them when the best time to speak over the phone would be. Be polite and tell them you are excited to start working there.

Of course, do not burn any bridges at your old job either. Many software developers I have met worked for companies that would not let them switch to the IT department while they were working there, only to offer them great packages after they had some developer experience at another company.

Conclusion

You are in the final stretch! Do not rush any decisions right now. You want to take the job offer that is right for you now and for your career in the future. Remember that you are creating value for the company. At first, the company might not see you as providing much value versus the risk that they are taking on for hiring you - a new developer with no track record of performance. Soon, you will have experience, and everyone will realize the value that you can provide.

26

YOUR FIRST FEW WEEKS

"The day you stop learning is the day you begin decaying."

— Isaac Asimov, Famous Author

Congratulations on landing your first job in the industry! While it is a huge accomplishment, the work doesn't stop here. You are still new and need to prove yourself to the company that is taking a chance on hiring you as a new developer.

The first few days will be like any other job; filling out paperwork, going through HR training session, and making sure you get acquainted with the workplace. You will also start setting up your local environment. There will be apps to install and accounts to create. Other team members will show you how the development process works and help you get their code running on your local machine. Some companies will loan you a laptop and some will let you use your own. If your laptop is too old, then you can ask for assistance in getting a new one.

I recommend taking the first week and trying to look

through their codebase line by line, if you can. Ask lots of questions. Be upfront with any concepts or areas of the code you are struggling with. Have them help you find an easy task so you can contribute to the codebase within your first week or two. This will help you build momentum and be successful.

If they have you pair program as part of your training, make sure that you are not working with someone else incessantly. You need to build up the confidence work on your own, and becoming reliant on your partner can hinder your individual development.

Starting at a new job can be overwhelming, and remember to take care of your physical and mental health. It is not easy to sit at a desk solving problems all day. Get up and walk around to give your body and mind a break. I set my timer for every hour to remember to get up and stretch, breathe, and clear my head.

Try to build good relationships with your coworkers, but keep it professional. Your current co-workers might be good network opportunities for many future jobs. The preferred way for many companies to hire is through the networks of current employees.

Remember that you can be let go at any time, so set yourself up for long-term success by continuing to network and build your portfolio. Brand yourself as a thought leader and you will never have trouble finding another job.

Standing out

Even if they are assigning you easy tasks at the beginning, it is not the time to take it easy. You should be trying to impress them. Keep learning and grinding. The only difference now is that much of your learning is going to come during work hours. They are essentially paying you to learn now!

Remember that it is okay to take risks, speak up, volunteer for assignments, and be creative. Your mental energy is what they are paying you for and you will be come much more valuable to the team if you contribute your ideas.

The biggest piece of advice I can give you now is to be proactive in asking for help. From my experience, the number one reason that new developers fail at their job is lack of communication. Sometimes this is the result of arrogance, but usually it is more from not know when or how to ask questions and getting overwhelmed without letting anyone know about it.

The company that hired you knows that you are a new developer, so they have to expect a certain level of handholding initially. Make sure you are asking lots of questions and communicating where you are at on every tasks at the daily meetings. A good rule of thumb is to "communicate early and often."

27

CONCLUSION

> "If one advances confidently in the direction of his dreams, and endeavors to live the life which he has imagined, he will meet with a success unexpected in common hours."
>
> — Henry David Thoreau, Author

Thank you for purchasing this book. It truly makes me happy to know that you made it all the way to the end. If you follow the steps I outline in the book, you will soon have your first developer job. Someday, you will even have people reaching out to you asking to hire you.

Please continue the conversation with me by joining my Discord server listed on the contact page of my blog, gwenfaraday.com/contact. I am active there throughout the week talking about various aspects of software development and the tech industry.

I wish you success in your journey and I look forward to hearing your stories about how you got hired as a developer!

APPENDIX A - REFERENCES

Chapter 1

Stack overflow survey 2018: insights. stackoverflow.com/survey/2018

Stack overflow survey 2019: insights. stackoverflow.com/survey/2019

Github's yearly report, State of the Octoverse: octoverse.github.com

Chapter 3

State of JavaScript survey: 2018.stateofjs.com

Chapter 5

Spaced Repetition Learning Podcast Episode with Erez Zukerman: learnwithus.simplecast.com/episodes/erez-zukerman

Chapter 7

Clean Code, by Robert C. Martin: www.amazon.com/Clean-Code-Handbook-Software-Craftsmanship/dp/0132350882

How to Think Like a Programmer, by Any Harris: youtube.com/watch?v=YWwBhjQN-Qw

Chapter 9

Imposter Syndrome, by Socratica: https://www.youtube.com/watch?v=JtGBDv1Jwmc

Chapter 15

LinkedIn Talent Trends 2019: news.linkedin.com/2019/January/linkedin-releases-2019-global-talent-trends-report

Networking is the best way to get hired: www.forbes.com/sites/susanadams/2011/06/07/networking-is-still-the-best-way-to-find-a-job-survey-says/#8b58c2843661

Chapter 19

Creating a Github Profile README: docs.github.com/en/free-pro-team@latest/github/setting-up-and-managing-your-github-profile/managing-your-profile-readme

Chapter 20

Applying to jobs early in the morning: talent.works/2017/10/19/youre-5x-more-likely-to-get-job-interview-if-you-apply-by-10am

Finding jobs online: www.bls.gov/opub/mlr/2017/beyond-bls/online-job-search-the-new-normal.htm

Chapter 21

Inappropriate job questions: www.gsworkplace.lbl.gov/DocumentArchive/BrownBagLunches/IllegalorInappropriateInterviewQuestions.pdf

Interview questions that discriminate against females:

employment.findlaw.com/hiring-process/illegal-interview-questions-and-female-applicants.html

Chapter 22

Sheryl Sandberg's negotiating advice for women: www.inc.com/jessica-stillman/sheryl-sandbergs-best-negotiating-advice-for-women-is-only-2-words-long.html

APPENDIX B - RECOMMENDED RESOURCES

Books I Recommend Right Now

- *Getting Things Done: The Art of Stress-Free Productivity* by David Allan
- *Soft skills* by John Sonmez
- *No Degree, No Problem* by Josh Kemp

Books I Recommend After your First Thousand Hours of Coding

- *Clean Code: A Handbook of Agile Software Craftsmanship* by Robert C. Martin
- *The Pragmatic Programmer: From Journeyman to Master* by Andrew Hunt and David Thomas
- *Cracking the Coding Interview* by Gayle McDowell

Resources I Recommend

- Algorithms
- freeCodeCamp
- Code Wars
- HackerRank
- Khan Academy course on algorithms

▪ Blogs

- Faraday Academy (the author's blog)

- freeCodeCamp News

- Hackernoon

▪ Curriculum

- freeCodeCamp

- Grace Hopper Academy (it's a paid program, but they have a good curriculum that you can copy from even if you aren't going to attend as a student)

▪ Mailing Lists

- Faraday Academy Weekly Newsletter (the author's newsletter)

- freeCodeCamp Weekly Newsletter

▪ Podcasts

- Code Newbie

- freeCodeCamp

- Learn to Code with Me

▪ Programming Groups

- Facebook Groups

- Meetup

ABOUT THE AUTHOR

Gwendolyn Faraday is a senior software engineer, technical writer, and content creator from the United States of America. She has spent over five years running a coding group that encourages, supports, and teaches beginners software engineering skills. She has also given technical talks and workshops about various programming topics all over the world.

The topic of this book is of particular interest to her, being that she is a self-taught programmer and has also witnessed the struggles of many others that she has taught, mentored, and met throughout the years.

Contact Information

Twitter: @faradayacademy
Email: contact@faradayacademy.com

www.ingramcontent.com/pod-product-compliance
Lightning Source LLC
Chambersburg PA
CBHW031236050326
40690CB00007B/827
* 9 7 8 1 7 3 4 0 0 4 4 2 7 *